UNIX® Programming For Dummies®

P9-CRY-546

Writing UNIX Code

To Do This	Follow This Example
Display text on the screen	`echo "Place text here."`
Declare a variable	`set VariableName`
Assign a value to a string variable	`set VariableName = "Bob"`
Assign a value to a numeric variable	`@ VariableName = 500`
Display a variable	`echo "$VariableName"`
Save data to a file (instead of to the screen)	`echo "VariableName" > file`
Append data to a file (instead of to the screen)	`echo "VariableName" >> file`
Comment on a program	`#Written by John Grace`
Disable an instruction	`#set VariableName = "Bob"`

Check out the manual

If you want to know more about a UNIX utility, use the on-screen manual. For example, if you want to know more about the `sort` utility, type the following at the UNIX prompt and press Enter:

```
man sort
```

If the manual pages scroll off the screen, use the `more` command so that you can see one screen at a time.

```
man sort | more
```

Making decisions and repeating instructions

switch case

```
switch (VariableName)
case value1:
        Instruction
        breaksw

case value2:
        Instruction
        breaksw
endsw
```

Beginning with the `switch` reserved word and ending with the `endsw` reserved word, your program looks at the value of `VariableName`. If this value is equal to `value1`, the program follows the first set of instructions. If this is equal to `value2`, the program follows the second set of instructions. The program follows all the instructions that appear between the `case` reserved word and the `breaksw` reserved word if there is a match.

UNIX® Programming For Dummies®

Cheat Sheet

Making decisions and repeating instructions (continued)

while

```
while (Condition)
        Instruction
end
```

The `Condition` must be a variable or expression that results in a true or false value.

foreach

```
foreach VariableName (wordlist)
        Instruction
end
```

The `wordlist` is a list of string values that are assigned to the `VariableName`. The `VariableName` can be used by the instruction inside the `foreach` loop.

if

```
if (Condition)then
        Instruction
endif
```

Your program follows the `Instruction` if a certain `Condition` exists — meaning the `Condition` is true.

if else

```
if (Condition)then
        Instruction1
else
        Instruction2
endif
```

Your program obeys the first group of instructions if the `Condition` is true ... but obeys the second group of instructions if the `Condition` is false.

if else if

```
if (Condition1)then
        Instruction1
else if (Condition2)then
        Instruction2
endif
```

Your program obeys the first group of instructions if `Condition1` is true. However, if `Condition1` is false, your program determines if `Condition2` is true. If `Condition2` is true, your program obeys the second group of instructions. If `Condition2` is false, your program skips the second group of instructions.

IDG BOOKS WORLDWIDE

...For Dummies: #1 Computer Book Series for Beginners

®

References for the Rest of Us! ®

COMPUTER BOOK SERIES FROM IDG

Are you intimidated and confused by computers? Do you find that traditional manuals are overloaded with technical details you'll never use? Do your friends and family always call you to fix simple problems on their PCs? Then the *...For Dummies*® computer book series from IDG Books Worldwide is for you.

...For Dummies books are written for those frustrated computer users who know they aren't really dumb but find that PC hardware, software, and indeed the unique vocabulary of computing make them feel helpless. *...For Dummies* books use a lighthearted approach, a down-to-earth style, and even cartoons and humorous icons to diffuse computer novices' fears and build their confidence. Lighthearted but not lightweight, these books are a perfect survival guide for anyone forced to use a computer.

Already, hundreds of thousands of satisfied readers agree. They have made *...For Dummies* books the #1 introductory level computer book series and have written asking for more. So, if you're looking for the most fun and easy way to learn about computers, look to *...For Dummies* books to give you a helping hand.

™

IDG BOOKS
WORLDWIDE

UNIX®
PROGRAMMING
FOR
DUMMIES®

by Jim Keogh

IDG Books Worldwide, Inc.
An International Data Group Company

Foster City, CA ♦ Chicago, IL ♦ Indianapolis, IN ♦ Southlake, TX

UNIX® Programming For Dummies®

Published by
IDG Books Worldwide, Inc.
An International Data Group Company
919 E. Hillsdale Blvd.
Suite 400
Foster City, CA 94404
www.idgbooks.com (IDG Books Worldwide Web Site)
http://www.dummies.com (Dummies Press Web Site)

Library of Congress Catalog Card No.: 96-079282

ISBN: 0-7645-0061-9

Printed in the United States of America

10 9 8 7 6 5 4 3 2 1

1DD/RT/RR/ZW/IN

Distributed in the United States by IDG Books Worldwide, Inc.

Distributed by Macmillan Canada for Canada; by Contemporanea de Ediciones for Venezuela; by Distribuidora Cuspide for Argentina; by CITEC for Brazil; by Ediciones ZETA S.C.R. Ltda. for Peru; by Editorial Limusa SA for Mexico; by Transworld Publishers Limited in the United Kingdom and Europe; by Academic Bookshop for Egypt; by Levant Distributors S.A.R.L. for Lebanon; by Al Jassim for Saudi Arabia; by Simron Pty. Ltd. for South Africa; by Pustak Mahal for India; by The Computer Bookshop for India; by Toppan Company Ltd. for Japan; by Addison Wesley Publishing Company for Korea; by Longman Singapore Publishers Ltd. for Singapore, Malaysia, Thailand, and Indonesia; by Unalis Corporation for Taiwan; by WS Computer Publishing Company, Inc. for the Philippines; by WoodsLane Pty. Ltd. for Australia; by WoodsLane Enterprises Ltd. for New Zealand. Authorized Sales Agent: Anthony Rudkin Associates for the Middle East and North Africa.

For general information on IDG Books Worldwide's books in the U.S., please call our Consumer Customer Service department at 800-762-2974. For reseller information, including discounts and premium sales, please call our Reseller Customer Service department at 800-434-3422.

For information on where to purchase IDG Books Worldwide's books outside the U.S., please contact our International Sales department at 415-655-3172 or fax 415-655-3295.

For information on foreign language translations, please contact our Foreign & Subsidiary Rights department at 415-655-3021 or fax 415-655-3281.

For sales inquiries and special prices for bulk quantities, please contact our Sales department at 415-655-3200 or write to the address above.

For information on using IDG Books Worldwide's books in the classroom or for ordering examination copies, please contact our Educational Sales department at 800-434-2086 or fax 817-251-8174.

For authorization to photocopy items for corporate, personal, or educational use, please contact Copyright Clearance Center, 222 Rosewood Drive, Danvers, MA 01923, or fax 508-750-4470.

is a trademark under exclusive license to IDG Books Worldwide, Inc., from International Data Group, Inc.

About the Author

Jim Keogh

Jim Keogh is a professor of computer science at Saint Peter's College in Jersey City, New Jersey. He has developed UNIX systems for major Wall Street firms and is the author of more than 30 books on computers. He is a former columnist and contributing editor to *Popular Electronics Magazine* and associate editor for *Personal Computing Magazine*.

ABOUT IDG BOOKS WORLDWIDE

Welcome to the world of IDG Books Worldwide.

IDG Books Worldwide, Inc., is a subsidiary of International Data Group, the world's largest publisher of computer-related information and the leading global provider of information services on information technology. IDG was founded more than 25 years ago and now employs more than 8,500 people worldwide. IDG publishes more than 275 computer publications in over 75 countries (see listing below). More than 60 million people read one or more IDG publications each month.

Launched in 1990, IDG Books Worldwide is today the #1 publisher of best-selling computer books in the United States. We are proud to have received eight awards from the Computer Press Association in recognition of editorial excellence and three from *Computer Currents*' First Annual Readers' Choice Awards. Our best-selling *...For Dummies*® series has more than 30 million copies in print with translations in 30 languages. IDG Books Worldwide, through a joint venture with IDG's Hi-Tech Beijing, became the first U.S. publisher to publish a computer book in the People's Republic of China. In record time, IDG Books Worldwide has become the first choice for millions of readers around the world who want to learn how to better manage their businesses.

Our mission is simple: Every one of our books is designed to bring extra value and skill-building instructions to the reader. Our books are written by experts who understand and care about our readers. The knowledge base of our editorial staff comes from years of experience in publishing, education, and journalism — experience we use to produce books for the '90s. In short, we care about books, so we attract the best people. We devote special attention to details such as audience, interior design, use of icons, and illustrations. And because we use an efficient process of authoring, editing, and desktop publishing our books electronically, we can spend more time ensuring superior content and spend less time on the technicalities of making books.

You can count on our commitment to deliver high-quality books at competitive prices on topics you want to read about. At IDG Books Worldwide, we continue in the IDG tradition of delivering quality for more than 25 years. You'll find no better book on a subject than one from IDG Books Worldwide.

John Kilcullen
President and CEO
IDG Books Worldwide, Inc.

Eighth Annual Computer Press Awards ≥1992

Ninth Annual Computer Press Awards ≥1993

Tenth Annual Computer Press Awards ≥1994

Eleventh Annual Computer Press Awards ≥1995

IDG Books Worldwide, Inc., is a subsidiary of International Data Group, the world's largest publisher of computer-related information and the leading global provider of information services on information technology. International Data Group publishes over 275 computer publications in over 75 countries. Sixty million people read one or more International Data Group publications each month. International Data Group's publications include: **ARGENTINA:** Buyer's Guide, Computerworld Argentina, PC World Argentina; **AUSTRALIA:** Australian Macworld, Australian PC World, Australian Reseller News, Computerworld, IT Casebook, Network World, Publish, Webmaster; **AUSTRIA:** Computerwelt Osterreich, Networks Austria, PC Tip Austria; **BANGLADESH:** PC World Bangladesh; **BELARUS:** PC World Belarus; **BELGIUM:** Data News; **BRAZIL:** Annuário de Informática, Computerworld, Connections, Macworld, PC Player, PC World, Publish, Reseller News, Supergamepower; **BULGARIA:** Computerworld Bulgaria, Network World Bulgaria, PC & MacWorld Bulgaria; **CANADA:** CIO Canada, Client/Server World, ComputerWorld Canada, InfoWorld Canada, NetworkWorld Canada, WebWorld; **CHILE:** Computerworld Chile, PC World Chile; **COLOMBIA:** Computerworld Colombia, PC World Colombia; **COSTA RICA:** PC World Centro America; **THE CZECH AND SLOVAK REPUBLICS:** Computerworld Czechoslovakia, Macworld Czech Republic, PC World Czechoslovakia; **DENMARK:** Communications World Danmark, Computerworld Danmark, Macworld Danmark, PC World Danmark, Techworld Denmark; **DOMINICAN REPUBLIC:** PC World Republica Dominicana; **ECUADOR:** PC World Ecuador; **EGYPT:** Computerworld Middle East, PC World Middle East; **EL SALVADOR:** PC World Centro America; **FINLAND:** MikroPC, Tietoverkko, Tietoviikko; **FRANCE:** Distributique, Hebdo, Info PC, Le Monde Informatique, Macworld, Reseaux & Telecoms, WebMaster France; **GERMANY:** Computer Partner, Computerwoche, Computerwoche Extra, Computerwoche FOCUS, Global Online, Macwelt, PC Welt; **GREECE:** Amiga Computing, GamePro Greece, Multimedia World; **GUATEMALA:** PC World Centro America; **HONDURAS:** PC World Centro America; **HONG KONG:** Computerworld Hong Kong, PC World Hong Kong, Publish in Asia; **HUNGARY:** ABCD CD-ROM, Computerworld Szamitastechnika, Internetto online Magazine, PC World Hungary, PC-X Magazin Hungary; **ICELAND:** Tolvuheimur PC World Island; **INDIA:** Information Communications World, Information Systems Computerworld, PC World India, Publish in Asia; **INDONESIA:** InfoKomputer PC World, Komputek Computerworld, Publish in Asia; **IRELAND:** ComputerScope, PC Live!; **ISRAEL:** Macworld Israel, People & Computers/Computerworld; **ITALY:** Computerworld Italia, Macworld Italia, Networking Italia, PC World Italia; **JAPAN:** DTP World, Macworld Japan, Nikkei Personal Computing, OS/2 World Japan, SunWorld Japan, Windows NT World, Windows World Japan; **KENYA:** PC World East African; **KOREA:** Hi-Tech Information, Macworld Korea, PC World Korea; **MACEDONIA:** PC World Macedonia; **MALAYSIA:** Computerworld Malaysia, PC World Malaysia, Publish in Asia; **MALTA:** PC World Malta; **MEXICO:** Computerworld Mexico, PC World Mexico; **MYANMAR:** PC World Myanmar; **NETHERLANDS:** Computer! Totaal, LAN Internetworking Magazine, LAN World Buyers Guide, Macworld Netherlands, Net, WebWereld; **NEW ZEALAND:** Absolute Beginners Guide and Plain & Simple Series, Computer Buyer, Computer Industry Directory, Computerworld New Zealand, MTB, Network World, PC World New Zealand; **NICARAGUA:** PC World Centro America; **NORWAY:** Computerworld Norge, CW Rapport, Datamagasinet, Financial Rapport, Kursguide Norge, Macworld Norge, Multimediaworld Norge, PC World Ekspress Norge, PC World Nettverk, PC World Norge, PC World ProduktGuide Norge; **PAKISTAN:** Computerworld Pakistan; **PANAMA:** PC World Panama; **PEOPLE'S REPUBLIC OF CHINA:** China Computer Users, China Computerworld, China InfoWorld, China Telecom World Weekly, Computer & Communication, Electronic Design China, Electronics Today, Electronics Weekly, Game Software, PC World China, Popular Computer Week, Software Weekly, Software World, Telecom World; **PERU:** Computerworld Peru, PC World Profesional Peru, PC World SoHo Peru; **PHILIPPINES:** Click!, Computerworld Philippines, PC World Philippines, Publish in Asia; **POLAND:** Computerworld Poland, Computerworld Special Report Poland, Cyber, Macworld Poland, Networld Poland, PC World Komputer; **PORTUGAL:** Cerebro/PC World, Computerworld/Correio Informático, Dealer World Portugal, Mac*In/PC*In Portugal, Multimedia World; **PUERTO RICO:** PC World Puerto Rico; **ROMANIA:** Computerworld Romania, PC World Romania, Telecom Romania; **RUSSIA:** Computerworld Russia, Mir PK, Publish, Seti; **SINGAPORE:** Computerworld Singapore, PC World Singapore, Publish in Asia; **SLOVENIA:** Monitor; **SOUTH AFRICA:** Computing SA, Network World SA, Software World SA; **SPAIN:** Communicaciones World España, Computerworld España, Dealer World España, Macworld España, PC World España; **SRI LANKA:** Infolink PC World; **SWEDEN:** CAP&Design, Computer Sweden, Corporate Computing Sweden, Internetworld Sweden, it.branschen, Macworld Sweden, MaxiData Sweden, MikroDatorn, Nätverk & Kommunikation, PC World Sweden, PCaktiv, Windows World Sweden; **SWITZERLAND:** Computerworld Schweiz, Macworld Schweiz, PCtip; **TAIWAN:** Computerworld Taiwan, Macworld Taiwan, NEW ViSiON/Publish, PC World Taiwan; **THAILAND:** Publish in Asia, Thai Computerworld; **TURKEY:** Computerworld Turkiye, Macworld Turkiye, Network World Turkiye, PC World Turkiye; **UKRAINE:** Computerworld Kiev, Multimedia World Ukraine, PC World Ukraine; **UNITED KINGDOM:** Acorn User UK, Amiga Action UK, Amiga Computing UK, Apple Talk UK Computing, Macworld, Parents and Computers UK, PC Advisor, PC Home, PSX Pro, The WEB; **UNITED STATES:** Cable in the Classroom, CIO Magazine, Computerworld, DOS World, Federal Computer Week, GamePro Magazine, InfoWorld, I-Way, Macworld, Network World, PC Games, PC World, Publish, Video Event, THE WEB Magazine, and WebMaster; online webzines: JavaWorld, NetscapeWorld, and SunWorld Online; **URUGUAY:** InfoWorld Uruguay; **VENEZUELA:** Computerworld Venezuela, PC World Venezuela; and **VIETNAM:** PC World Vietnam.
10/22/96

Dedication

This book is dedicated to Anne, Sandra, and Joanne, without whose help this book wouldn't have been possible.

Publisher's Acknowledgments

We're proud of this book; please send us your comments about it by using the Reader Response Card at the back of the book or by e-mailing us at `feedback/dummies@idgbooks.com`. Some of the people who helped bring this book to market include the following:

Acquisitions, Development, and Editorial

Project Editor: Bill Helling

Assistant Acquisitions Editor: Gareth Hancock

Copy Editors: Rebecca Whitney, Joe Jansen, John C. Edwards

Technical Editor: John Baldino

Editorial Manager: Mary C. Corder

Editorial Assistant: Chris H. Collins

Production

Project Coordinator: Regina Snyder

Layout and Graphics: E. Shawn Aylsworth, Brett Black, Cameron Booker, Elizabeth Cárdenas-Nelson, J. Tyler Connor, Dominique DeFelice, Maridee V. Ennis, Angela F. Hunckler, Todd Klemme, Jane E. Martin, Drew R. Moore, Anna C. Rohrer, Brent Savage, Kate Snell, Michael Sullivan

Proofreaders: Rachel Garvey, Nancy Price, Robert Springer, Carrie Voorhis, Karen York

Indexer: Sharon Hilgenberg

General and Administrative

IDG Books Worldwide, Inc.: John Kilcullen, President and CEO; Steven Berkowitz, COO and Publisher

Dummies, Inc.: Milissa Koloski, Executive Vice President and Publisher

Dummies Technology Press and Dummies Editorial: Diane Graves Steele, Vice President and Associate Publisher; Judith A. Taylor, Brand Manager

Dummies Trade Press: Kathleen A. Welton, Vice President and Publisher; Stacy S. Collins, Brand Manager

IDG Books Production for Dummies Press: Beth Jenkins, Production Director; Cindy L. Phipps, Supervisor of Project Coordination; Kathie S. Schutte, Supervisor of Page Layout; Shelley Lea, Supervisor of Graphics and Design; Debbie J. Gates, Production Systems Specialist; Tony Augsburger, Reprint Coordinator; Leslie Popplewell, Media Archive Coordinator

Dummies Packaging and Book Design: Patti Sandez, Packaging Assistant; Kavish+Kavish, Cover Design

◆

The publisher would like to give special thanks to Patrick J. McGovern, without whom this book would not have been possible.

◆

Author's Acknowledgments

I would like to thank John Baldino's contribution through his timely technical edits.

Cartoons at a Glance

By Rich Tennant • Fax: 508-546-7747 • E-mail: the5wave@tiac.net

The 5th Wave — By Rich Tennant

Re·al Pro·gram·mers

Real Programmers code in pen.

page 7

The 5th Wave — By Rich Tennant

"OOPS - HERE'S THE PROBLEM. SOMETHING'S CAUSING SHORTS IN THE GOPHER SERVER."

page 43

The 5th Wave — By Rich Tennant

Re·al Pro·gram·mers

Real Programmers strive to insult users with error messages.

page 115

The 5th Wave — By Rich Tennant

It's really made the job a lot less complicated! Oh jeez—now what?

page 165

The 5th Wave — By Rich Tennant

"YEAH, I USED TO WORK ON REFRIGERATORS, WASHING MACHINES, STUFF LIKE THAT- HOW'D YOU GUESS?"

page 201

The 5th Wave — By Rich Tennant

WELL HOT DANG!! FINALLY—A FAULT TOLERANT PRETZEL MAKER THAT RUNS UNDER UNIX!

LARRY'S HOMEMADE PRETZELS

LARRY'S HOMEMADE PRETZELS

page 51

The 5th Wave — By Rich Tennant

Re·al Pro·gram·mers

ELEVATOR CAPACITY 2000 LBS.

Real Programmers love to talk "computer-eze" while ordinary citizens are listening.

page 93

The 5th Wave — By Rich Tennant

Re·al Pro·gram·mers

Real Programmers don't sleep - their systems just temporarily go down.

page 229

The 5th Wave — By Rich Tennant

page 139

Contents at a Glance

Table of Contents

Appendix B: When The Moon Hits Your Eye Like a Big Piece of vi 241

Introduction

● ●

*W*elcome to the world of UNIX programming. Just the thought of programming a computer is enough to make most people give up immediately because it usually seems too complicated. Clear your mind of that myth — it ain't that difficult.

Can you write a grocery list or directions to your house? Of course you can! You can also write a UNIX program (seriously!).

This book is not like the other computer books you may have attempted to read. Most of the confusing technical jargon has been scrapped. In its place, I have put some honest-to-goodness common-sense English words that tell you how to make a computer do what you want it to do.

Writing instructions to tell a computer to do something doesn't have to be difficult. After you find out how to perform a few simple tricks, computer programming is a great deal of fun.

The pages of this book are filled with simple explanations for things you may have believed required an engineering degree to understand. I provide plenty of examples for you to copy and try out on your computer.

About This Book

Pretend that this book is your private tutor who comes to your home to make sure that you understand how to write a program in UNIX. Programming in UNIX isn't difficult, but sometimes it requires that you provide many small details to tell your computer how to do something.

Here are a few samples of the subjects I discuss in *UNIX Programming For Dummies:*

  ✔ Planning a UNIX program

  ✔ Developing the user interface

  ✔ Understanding what UNIX code can do

You may think that understanding how to program a computer requires you to take technical courses in abstract mathematics at your local college. You're wrong. The purpose of this book is to walk you through all the steps you need to know in order to write a UNIX program so that you can leave the pain behind.

How to Use This Book

In this book, you read the procedures for creating a user interface for your programs, and then you can begin to write the UNIX code that tells the computer how to respond to someone who uses your programs.

All the code in this book is set in monospace type, like this:

```
set VariableName
```

You should type, character for character, anything that appears. I'll tell you when you need to make substitutions, such as using a real variable name in place of `VariableName`. UNIX cares about whether you use uppercase, lowercase, or a mixture of uppercase and lowercase letters, so look closely at any code that you see.

Because of the length of the margins in this book, some long lines of code may wrap to the next line. On your computer, however, these wrapped lines are displayed as a single line of code; be sure not to insert a hard return when you see one of them on-screen.

Tests are sprinkled throughout this book. Don't get too concerned — just use them to test your knowledge (no grades are given). You will know immediately how you're doing because only one answer is correct; the other answers are outrageously wrong.

Foolish Assumptions

Here are some things you should be sure to know how to do before you read this book:

- Turn your computer on and off
- Type words on the keyboard
- Read

But seriously, remember that this is a UNIX programming book. You probably already know what a bug is, what a command line is, and so on. I don't think you are someone who has never even touched a computer. I bet you may have read *DOS For Dummies* or perhaps *Windows For Dummies* — maybe even *UNIX For Dummies* (all from IDG Books Worldwide, Inc.) You may even be a programmer who wants to learn UNIX programming.

However, even if you have no previous knowledge, you should still be able to follow along. You don't have to know how a computer works, and you don't have to have a high SAT score. A little common sense is the only requirement to understand what's in this book.

Of course, you also need a computer that is running UNIX. And I wrote this book with the C shell in mind (I discuss the C shell in Chapter 3), which is just one of the many shells available for UNIX. But even if you are using another shell (such as the Bourne shell or the Korn shell), don't despair. In Appendix C, I give you a table of equivalent commands.

If you qualify and have the guts to continue, get ready for an interesting and fun adventure into the creation of UNIX programs for your computer.

How This Book Is Organized

This book is composed of nine parts, and each part usually consists of several chapters. If you've had no programming experience, a lot of the material in this book will make more sense to you if you read the chapters in order. But if you have a little previous knowledge and can figure some things out, feel free to just pick up this book and start anywhere.

Here's a breakdown of the parts and what you can read about in them:

Part I: A Beginner's Introduction to UNIX Programming

Part I is a brief introduction to all the major features of UNIX programming. This part of the book is the place to begin to help relieve your fears about programming a computer.

Part II: The Basics of Writing Code

To find out how to write a UNIX program that tells the computer to do something, read Part II. It helps you understand how to use the UNIX shell script language to give instructions to the computer.

Part III: Making Decisions

Part III tells you how to instruct your computer to make up its own mind about performing a task and then do something special without asking for additional directions. Your instructions, in effect, let your computer become self-reliant.

Part IV: Loops and Loops

Loops are another way of telling your computer to continue doing something until it gets it right. In Part IV, you read about different ways to make your computer repeat itself.

Part V: Writing Subprograms

Just the thought of writing a large computer program is enough to make any sane person run far away. Part V shows you the tricks of how to break down a large program into many smaller programs called subprograms.

Part VI: Database Programs and Printing

Database programs are special programs your computer uses to store and retrieve information in a file on your hard disk. In Part VI, you learn how a computer handles that information. You also discover how to print any information on paper.

Part VII: Debugging Your Program

In this small part, you find out the tried-and-true ways of tracking down a problem in your UNIX program. It's not as complicated as it sounds!

Part VIII: The Part of Tens

Part VIII contains several chapters of miscellaneous information that you may find useful and interesting, including tips about UNIX utilities you can use with your programs.

Part IX: Appendixes

This part contains some helpful appendixes. Here you can find a glossary of terms, a section on using the vi text editor, and information on the differences in writing scripts with other UNIX shells. I also include an appendix with plenty of UNIX programming exercises — with answers!

Icons Used in This Book

Denotes technical details that are informative (and sometimes interesting) but not necessary to know about. Skip these areas if you want.

Flags useful or helpful information that makes programming even less complicated.

Indicates important information — don't pass up these gentle reminders.

Alerts you to something you shouldn't do. Proceed cautiously when you encounter this icon.

Points out places where you test your newfound knowledge. Relax. I guarantee that you can pass these tests without even reading the chapter. And if you do read the chapter, so much the better for you!

Where to Go from Here

Now it's time to launch your exploration into the world of UNIX programming. Grab a comfortable chair, sit back, and get ready to have some fun.

Part I

A Beginner's Introduction to UNIX Programming

The 5th Wave By Rich Tennant

Re'al Pro·gram·mers

Real Programmers code in pen.

In this part . . .

If you felt that the great paying jobs are given to computer programmers and you're not one because computer programming seems too complicated, this book is for you.

You heard about computer programming at work or on television, and you heard that the kids in your old high school know how to do it. You'd like to give it a try, but you don't know where to begin.

Guess what? You have already started when you opened this book. You won't find pages of technical computer jargon here. You will find the first steps you need begin programming a computer.

Chapter 1

How UNIX Programming Works

*T*he primary reason for writing a computer program is to make a computer do something useful. To begin writing a UNIX program, first turn off your computer and then use some paper and a pencil to plan exactly what you want to make the computer do.

You can make a computer do virtually anything you can imagine, short of making it take your driver's test or having it print money to pay your bills (although some people have used computers illegally to print money). A computer program can perform such basic tasks as display a few words on-screen or more complicated tasks, such as track an airplane flight across the country.

After you have determined what you want the computer to do, you must write down step-by-step instructions in a programming language to tell the computer how to do what you want.

Writing a UNIX Program

Just as millions of ways exist to earn money, millions of ways exist to write a computer program correctly. Some people work with their hands to make buildings, others draw up construction plans, and some folks spend their time trying to figure out how to marry into a wealthy family. Likewise, you can write the same computer program in an unlimited number of ways; no matter which way you write it, however, the result is always the same — a program.

Your job is that of a *programmer,* or the person who writes a computer program. You want to write programs that are easy to use, of course, and that correctly tell a computer what to do. No one can use a program that doesn't work correctly (although that won't stop you from selling your programs before you're run out of town) and a program that's difficult to use frustrates anyone who uses it and gets tossed in the garbage, even if it works fine.

To make sure that each program you write gets the job done, test it to make sure that you're on target. If a program is supposed to display names and addresses on-screen but prints names and addresses instead, it's obvious that the program doesn't work (unless you change what the program is supposed to do to printing names and addresses).

Deciding whether your program is easy to use, however, is a difficult job. What you think is easy can be an insurmountable task for someone else. Everyone knows, for example, how to board a bus, pay the fare, find a seat, and get off the bus at the right bus stop, even if she has never traveled on that particular bus line. The same concept applies when someone uses your UNIX program (if you have made it easy to use, of course). Users expect to start your program by typing the name of the program into the computer or choosing your program from a menu that appears on-screen. After your program is running, users expect menus that walk them through each step and screens that have a logical flow. The structure of your program should be similar to other programs and familiar to anyone who uses it.

Understanding the UNIX programming development cycle

Nine steps are necessary to create a UNIX program (the same number of innings necessary for a no-hitter in baseball — unless it's a rain-shortened game). The first eight steps are called the *development cycle:*

1. **Decide what you want the computer to do.**

2. **Decide how your program will look on-screen (the *user interface*).**

3. **Create the user interface by using common objects, such as text and areas in which users can enter information.**

4. **Arrange these common objects into a logical flow on one or more screens.**

5. **Write instructions in UNIX to make each part of the program do something.**

6. **Run the program to see whether it works.**

7. **When your program doesn't work, say out loud, "I hate computers!" (and then remember that computers do only what they are told to do).**

8. Look for errors (called *bugs*) in your program.

9. Start over. (Not optional.)

Don't plan to memorize these nine steps. Plan to follow them, however, every time you write a computer program. No shortcuts are available, and you cannot skip any steps. Skipping a step is similar to trying to run before you get out of bed, get dressed, and jump out on the sidewalk: You can move your legs as fast as they can move, but you won't get anywhere. (If you get tired of this fruitless effort, you can always just stop, roll over, and pull the covers over your head.)

Guess which step is the most difficult? The first step! When you know what you want a computer to do, you have to find a way to give the computer the correct instructions. The trick to completing this step is to lock yourself in a room with plenty of junk food and caffeine sources and then keep plugging away until you succeed.

A quick (and incomplete) history of the UNIX programming language

Before you begin to write UNIX programs, you might find it interesting to know where UNIX programming comes from.

Back in the 1960s, some Bell Labs employees set out to build a program that enabled a computer to become a *multitasking operating system,* or a operating system that runs more than one program at the same time. They used the same clever program to enable more than one person to use the same computer at the same time, which is called a *multiuser operating system.*

Guess what name was given to this brilliant program? UNIX!

UNIX is more than one program; it's a group of programs divided into three parts:

Kernel: Controls the parts of the computer, such as the hard disk, memory, and other stuff that makes the computer work

File system: Makes sure that your information doesn't get lost

Shell: Controls how the computer works

The Bell Labs folks also tried to make it easy to control a computer. They built many programs into UNIX, each of which does something well. These programs, called *utilities,* can sort information, search for information in a file, and perform a variety of other tasks. You learn more about utilities in "UNIX utilities already exist," later in this chapter.

Those computer whiz kids came up with a way to make building a program much easier than ever. Now programmers can combine just the utilities you need into a UNIX program called a *shell script.* This script makes it possible to write complex, sophisticated UNIX programs in just a short time. All the tricky stuff is already programmed into the utilities. You just have to choose the right ones and combine them into the programs you write.

By the 1980s, these UNIX features, in addition to the rapid creation of powerful and low-cost computers, brought UNIX from the halls of universities and the Department of Defense (DoD) into industry.

Developing the user interface

A *user interface* is simply the method used for giving commands to a computer when a program is running and then enabling the computer to respond. This interface is what a program displays on-screen, including which keys users must press in order to use the program.

The user interface in a UNIX program doesn't have the exploding screen or rainbow-colored windows you see in Microsoft Windows programs. Your creativity must create excitement from the sparse screens you can build in UNIX.

Don't use this limitation as a crutch! You still can create easy-to-use UNIX programs, even though you can't use all the bells and whistles a Windows program has.

Examining user-interface objects

A user interface in a UNIX program has two objects: the text and the cursor (where the user actually types something in), as shown here:

```
The Telephone Directory

1. Find a telephone number
2. Modify an existing telephone number
3. Add a new telephone number

Q Quit

Enter your selection:
```

Unlike Windows and the Mac, which are graphical-based environments, UNIX is a character-based environment.

UNIX displays only characters on-screen unless a fancy program such as Motif is running on the computer. (Motif makes UNIX look like Windows.) And you can't create in your UNIX programs any of the push buttons, drop-down list boxes, and other objects used by Windows and the Mac.

The folks at Bell Labs were concerned only about making UNIX easier for programmers, not ultraeasy for someone to use the program. Remember that because *you* are the UNIX programmer, you want to make it easier for the user.

More about pictures and characters (if you really must know)

In the olden days (do I sound like one of your grandparents?), when computers ran very slowly, computers could display characters on-screen fast in only one way: A program simply told the computer to display a letter on-screen ("Give me an E, give me a Y!"). The computer was smart enough to display the letter at the spot where the cursor was located.

Your computer screen is made up of tiny "lightbulb" dots called *pixels*. When you turn on the appropriate pixels, the letter *e* is displayed, for example.

A *character-based* system divides the screen into blocks of pixels called *character blocks*. A character block typically has 45 pixels (nine rows and five columns, but who's counting?). Your computer, not your program, controls which of the 45 pixels are lit.

A *graphics-based* system has no character blocks in it. Your program must light each pixel to form letters or any other image you want to appear on-screen.

Writing UNIX code

After you plan what you want your programs to do and how to make them easy for someone to use, you must write down your ideas in a way that a computer can understand what you want it to do. You must use instructions (also known as *code*) written in a computer language. You can use C, Pascal, or a UNIX shell script language (why else would you be reading this book?) to direct the computer to do what you have in mind.

1. **Decide which tasks you want the computer to perform.**

2. **Determine the order in which each task should be performed (it's similar to knowing that you have to stand upright before you begin running).**

3. **Find the correct commands in the shell script language that tell the computer which task you want performed.**

4. **Use a UNIX editor program (sort of an old word-processing program without the fancy features) to type all the commands into the shell script file in the order in which you want the computer to follow them. (I give my recommendations for a text editor in Chapter 3.)**

Stuff you probably don't want to know about programming languages

Your computer doesn't understand English or Spanish or any other spoken language, for that matter. The only language it understands is *binary code* (or *machine language*), which is composed of a bunch of zeros and ones. Try writing a program using this method, and you will head directly for the loony bin. Programmers are different from the average Joe, but they're not crazy, so some scientists created an "easier" programming language called an *assembly language*.

Before your computer can run the assembly language program, you have to call in the translator. Another program has to interpret assembly language into the zeros and ones your computer can read.

As in any translation, problems exist. For example, it takes longer to say certain things in one language than in another. And a computer language is no different. It takes longer to say the same thing in assembly language than it does in machine language. Therefore, assembly language programs end up being larger and slower than the same program written in machine language.

Because many programmers found assembly language difficult to use, the scientists went back to the drawing board and created new and improved languages, such as C, C++, Pascal, and BASIC. (The scientists created a number of other languages, but who cares?) The creators of each of these newfangled languages set out to make writing instructions for a computer to follow as easy as writing instructions to a friend.

Although not one computer language is as simple to use as your own mother language (English, Spanish, or whatever), the best computer language is the one that enables you to create a program in the shortest amount of time and with the fewest number of mistakes. Remember that because each of these fancy programming languages must be translated into machine language, you should avoid arguments over which is the better computer language to use.

The computer language your programs use isn't what makes the difference in their performance over similar programs. The competitive edge lies in the design of the programs and the efficiency of the program that performs the translation into machine language.

Many programmers forget that the translator program is the "programmer" that writes the actual instructions your computer executes. You don't have a choice about which translator program your program uses: If a translator isn't already installed on your computer, it's supplied with the computer language.

If you want to create an ultrafast program (and you're willing to go through the torture of writing it), learn how to use assembly language. Otherwise, stick with a language that's easier to use, such as BASIC or UNIX shell scripts. You can read more about shell scripts in the sidebar "A quick (and incomplete) history of the UNIX programming language," earlier in this chapter.

Giving a UNIX Program a Proper Name

A UNIX program can be saved in one file or in more than one file, depending on how many commands you need in order to tell the computer what you want it to do. You always need at least one file for any UNIX program.

Some computer languages, such as C and Visual Basic, require a project file that helps you keep track of your programs. UNIX programs, however, do not require any special file. There's nothing special, in fact, about the file that contains your UNIX program except how you name your program files.

Here are some guidelines and rules for choosing a filename:

- ✔ You can call the program file virtually any name you can imagine (although MoeLarryCurly is a little less than creative). Use some common sense, and make the name reflect the contents of the file (TelephoneList, JanBudget, or FamilyTree, for example).

- ✔ The file name has a limit of 14 characters. You can choose almost any 14 characters for the filename. You can use just one character if you want, but your filenames should be a little more descriptive. (How will you ever remember what's in a file named X?)

- ✔ Feel free to use a combination of upper- and lowercase letters in your filenames. UNIX doesn't change filenames into all uppercase letters, like DOS does.

- ✔ Do not use spaces or the following characters in your filenames (because your computer won't like you if you do):

  $! & ; | \ /

The following list shows variations for naming your files (although the names are similar, each file is actually different because UNIX is case sensitive):

- ✔ AddressList
- ✔ addresslist
- ✔ addressList
- ✔ Addresslist
- ✔ Address_List

Running a UNIX Program

You can run your UNIX program *almost* right away. You don't have to use another program to convert your UNIX program to machine language before you can use your program (machine language is described in the sidebar "Stuff you probably don't want to know about programming languages," earlier in this chapter). You get either instant gratification or pain (if the program doesn't work correctly).

Keep running your program over and over again until you stamp out those confounded bugs. In other words, fix all the problems with your program. Only then should you call all your co-workers over to see your new creation.

Making a file executable with the chmod utility

Your UNIX program files don't need any extensions, such as .EXE, .BAT, or .COM. (You can leave extensions to the DOS programs you write.) However, you do have to tell the computer that this is an *executable* file, that is, a file containing instructions for the computer to follow. You do this by using the chmod utility. For example, type the following at the prompt (replacing "myfile" with the name of your file, of course!):

```
chmod 711 myfile
```

If you don't make a file executable, UNIX doesn't recognize it as such. After you make a file executable, you can run the program by simply typing the name of the program at the command prompt.

What chmod 711 *actually means*

Your computer knows whether a file is a program by the permissions you grant to users of the file. A permission limits the accessibility to the file. You can grant three kinds of permissions to any file: read, write, and executable.

First decide who can use your program: the owner (you); the group (such as your friends who work with you); and others (everyone else in the world). You can grant individual permissions by placing the sum of permissions in the proper order in the chmod utility:

    owner   group   others

The first of the three numbers used with the chmod utility refers to the permission granted to the owner of the file. The second number identifies the permissions for the group. The third number tells the utility how to set the permissions for everyone else.

Here's how to grant the permissions you need. Each permission corresponds to one of these numbers:

- ✔ Read: 4
- ✔ Write: 2
- ✔ Executable: 1

Add the numbers, and then use the sum with the chmod utility. Say you want to make the file an executable file (a program file) but you also want to be able to read the file on the screen and change whatever you see; you'll need read and write permissions to do this stuff.

Add together the numbers assigned to each permission (4 + 2 + 1 = 7). 7 is the number you use with the chmod utility. However, if you just want to grant read and write permissions without making the file an executable file, you'd use the number 6 (4 + 2 = 6) with the chmod utility.

So chmod 711 myfile (where "myfile" is the name of the file you are assigning permissions to) means that the owner (you) has read, write, and executable permissions and that both the group and others can only execute your program.

UNIX Shell Script Languages versus Other Languages

Because writing a program in UNIX requires a different way of thinking than when you program in other computer languages, this section gives you some important features that are easy to overlook. They're here, at your fingertips, whenever you feel a lapse of memory coming on.

UNIX utilities already exist

In most programming languages, you first plan what you want the computer to do and then decide which instructions to give to make it happen. UNIX programming is a little different. You still must plan the task to get the job done, but most of the instructions are already written in the form of a UNIX utility. So divide your program into tasks you want the computer to perform, and then find the proper UNIX utility to do it. (Bell Labs created UNIX so that programmers can quickly assemble their programs from well-tested utilities. All you have to do is to choose the right utilities and put them in your program.)

Each utility requires input (that you supply). After the utility finishes working, it delivers output that can be used as input for another utility. As an example, a text editor utility creates a file that can be used as input to the spell check utility.

Learning how to use a UNIX utility could become a nightmare if not for this clever little trick: Most utilities have a how-to manual, called a *man page,* installed on any computer running UNIX (and, no, it's not a list of eligible men). Man is short for *man*ual. To display the manual on your computer screen, just type the following line (replacing "utility" with the utility name!) and then press Enter:

```
man utility
```

After you find a utility you want to use, test it out before you make it part of your program. Each utility is a program. Enter the name of the utility on the UNIX command line along with the input it needs. When you press the Enter key, the utility crunches away, and the output is displayed on-screen (unless the utility is supposed to send the output to a printer or modem).

UNIX reads, converts, and executes one line at a time

Most programs that you use on a PC have the .EXE extension. These letters in a filename tell DOS that the file is a program that's in machine language. (You can save any file with the .EXE extension, of course, but saving anything other than a program in this way only confuses your computer.) The computer can jump right into the program and follow your instructions as fast as a speeding bullet.

You don't get this same performance with UNIX programs. Programs written in most other computer languages are *compiled* (already in machine language before the program is run), but not so for UNIX. A *compiler* is a program that translates your program into machine language and then saves the translation in a file (the .EXE file in DOS). Your UNIX programs also must be translated into machine language, but this translation takes place when a user runs an executable program rather than when you create it.

The translation takes place one line at a time. Your computer reads one line of the UNIX shell script, converts the line into machine language, and then executes the instruction. Your computer goes back to your UNIX shell script, reads the next line, and follows the same steps. This process continues until your program ends. Translating your program line by line when you run the program can slow things down a little.

UNIX can run quietly in the background

Whenever you run a computer program, it takes over your computer: The program determines what appears on-screen and when you can use your keyboard.

Your UNIX program isn't a hog — it's willing to share your computer with other programs because UNIX is a multiprocessing operating system. Someone who has another program besides your program to run can tell the computer to run your program, and then other programs. Because your program just does its thing in the background, this process is called *background processing.*

The program you are currently using, called the *foreground process,* takes charge of everything you see on the computer screen. Any program that runs in UNIX is called a process because UNIX is processing the instructions and data that is associated with the program. A *daemon* — any program running in the background — is out there somewhere, too. After you launch your program as a daemon, it runs quietly somewhere in your computer's memory where only your computer can find it. It's easy to forget that the program is even running.

Any program can become a daemon if you type & (an ampersand) after the name of your program on the command line — which is the line on which the cursor rests, waiting for you to enter the next command or program name.

A daemon continues to run until you log off your computer, unless you started the program in a special way. (The only way to stop a daemon for good is to use the `kill` command.) You can run your UNIX program with the `nohup` command, however, which tells your computer to continue to run the program even after you log off the computer. Type the following (but replace "myprogram" with your program's name!):

```
nohup myprogram
```

UNIX uses subprograms

Whenever you write any type of program, you should break up what you want the computer to do into a series of tasks. Each task then becomes an individual part of the entire program. You can divide an address book program, for example, into segments that let you perform these separate tasks:

- ✔ Enter a new address
- ✔ Find an existing address
- ✔ Modify an existing address

In programming languages other than UNIX, each segment of a program is built separately from the other segments and then is assembled into the final program. None of the program segments (called procedures, functions, and subroutines in languages such as BASIC and C) can be executed by itself.

UNIX programming is somewhat different. The program is still divided into segments, but the segments are really smaller programs (called *subprograms*). Unlike the procedures, functions, and subroutines in other languages, each segment in UNIX can be run by itself or be called by another program.

A subprogram can be used a number of times within a program by simply calling the subprogram. You can save countless hours of programming time by reusing instructions in a subprogram. Then you don't have to write the instructions over again or spend time debugging. You write and debug instructions one time when the subprogram is created and then you call the subprogram when you need it in your program.

You must set the permissions for the subprograms your created as executable so that you can run them as part of your program. To find out about permissions, be sure to see "Running a UNIX Program," earlier in this chapter.

The drawbacks of UNIX programming

All the good parts of UNIX programming are balanced by factors that some UNIX programmers wish would change for the better (don't hold your breath, though). The UNIX environment is ideal for hackers and people who don't like the limitations of Microsoft Windows and the Mac (where the command line is hidden from you). For the rest of us, however, UNIX is a step backward.

Some people (such as Bill Gates) try to hide all the complicated stuff behind fancy windows. The folks at Bell Labs, however, designed UNIX so that you have to get hip-deep into the mess. Rather than just press buttons and choose items from pull-down menus like in Windows, anyone using a UNIX program (including yours) must type commands on the command line to get the program rolling (it sort of takes you back to the days of DOS and the Apple IIe in the 1970s and '80s).

To create the fancy screens users expect from professional programs, you must go beyond UNIX programming and learn how to program X-Windows (provides multiple windows on the screen), and Motif (supplies push buttons and scroll bars).

Another drawback of UNIX programming is the shell script language used to create programs. The words you use to tell a computer what to do are different in each computer language. You use different words in the C programming language to display your name on-screen, for example, than you use to do the same thing in BASIC. In UNIX programming, however, different words are used for the same instruction. The words you use in your UNIX program depend on the shell that interprets your script.

The *shell* is the program that translates commands entered by someone at the command line into instructions the computer can understand. Entering a command can be as simple as clearing the screen or translating each line of your program. UNIX has many shells: the *Bourne shell*, *C shell*, and *Korn shell* are just a few — whiz kids are creating new ones every day. (See Chapter 3 for more information on these three main shells.)

Because each shell has its own language, when you set out to write a UNIX program, you must decide which shell language to use. This problem doesn't exist in other operating systems because they have only *one* shell.

Test your newfound knowledge

1. What would be a bad name to give a file for a UNIX program?

    a. A cuddly animal name

    b. A name with spaces or characters such as $ and !

    c. A name that is hard for UNIX to pronounce

    d. A French name

2. How do you make a file executable for UNIX?

    a. Accuse it of treason.

    b. Tell everyone its secret name.

    c. Use the chmod utility.

    d. You never have to. UNIX anticipates your wants and needs.

Chapter 2

Designing Your First User Interface

● ●

In This Chapter

▶ Deciding how to tell users what to do in a UNIX program

▶ Creating a plan for your UNIX program to follow

▶ Mapping out your program's on-screen elements

● ●

*B*efore you can write your first UNIX program, you have to know how to make your program easy for someone else to use. You have to decide how users will interface with your program, choose which words to display on-screen, define the list of menu options, and then write the UNIX code.

Although programs are different from each other, most tend to work the same way because they have similar features. Programs display a menu, ask the user to make a selection, and then respond to the request. For example, every user interface shows information on-screen. Windows and Mac programs use a graphical user interface to display information, and UNIX programs use character blocks to display information. Both types of programs can practically display the same information on-screen.

When a user starts a program, the program displays options from which the user can choose in order to tell the computer what to do next (pick tomorrow's winning lottery number, for example). Windows and Mac programs present these options as *icons* (little pictures a user clicks with the mouse to issue a command), menu bar items, and other fancy techniques. UNIX programs display options in text format and simply ask you to press a corresponding key on your keyboard.

Instructions in a UNIX program are displayed on-screen to tell users what the program expects them to do next. The program is saying, in effect, "Come on, press one of those confounded keys!"

The UNIX shell language provides all the commonly used parts — display information, read the keyboard, and do something with the information read from the keyboard — of a typical UNIX program. A user just has to use the right words in the language to provide the correct instructions to the computer.

A short history of user interfaces

A long time ago, back when the '57 Chevy was new, computers weren't friendly. It was a downright dreadful task, in fact, to have to program a computer to do *anything*. You had to sit in front of a bunch of cables and a computer full of holes and then plug the correct cable into the correct hole, in much the same way as telephone operators do in those old movies.

Someone must have gotten electrocuted somewhere along the line because by the time Eisenhower was moving out of the White House (during the 1960s, for those of you who weren't born yet), the task of plugging in wires was eliminated. Paper, in the form of cards that resembled index cards, took the place of cables. Each task you wanted the computer to perform was represented by marking one of these *punch cards* with a series of holes (you could indicate only one task per card). In the final step, someone had to stack thousands of the punch cards in a precise order and then feed them into the computer.

By the time the Nixon era was winding down (during the 1970s — yes, this is a history quiz in disguise), someone had a bright idea: Get rid of punch cards! At the moment this brilliant person decided to use a keyboard and a television monitor to teach the computer to perform tasks, the modern-day user interface was born. When you turned on a computer, a blinking dot (and nothing else) was displayed. The dot implied that the computer was ready for its first command — no menus and no instructions appeared on-screen. You had to know that the appearance of the blinking dot meant that it was time to type a computer instruction on the keyboard. This command-line interface was displayed whenever the DOS prompt was displayed. To get a computer to do anything, however, you had to know the proper command to give to the computer (and how to spell the command correctly).

During the 1980s (the history quiz is over), as programmers transformed sparse screens into groups of choices users had to make, programs became *menu driven*. Some smart people (and you can soon be one of them) developed programs that seemed to demonstrate the best way to show menus on the screen.

Great! An easy way for anyone to use a program — except that no two programs worked the same way. Some brighter programmers set out to fix this problem (and made about a billion dollars) by throwing away the old computer manuals and making way for the *GUI,* or *graphical user interface.*

No, Bill Gates did not invent the GUI. Many programmers and companies, including Xerox and Apple Computer, had a hand in creating it. Gates just had the marketing clout to make the GUI popular.

Although UNIX programs were originally built by programmers for universities and the Department of Defense (DoD), its basic user interface hasn't progressed much beyond the command-line interface because most UNIX whiz kids are hackers who are comfortable with working with the command line.

UNIX has recently entered the GUI world, however, through add-on software such as X-Windows and Motif.

 You can do in your UNIX programs virtually anything that is done in one of those fancy Windows or Mac user interfaces. UNIX doesn't use *fancy* menus, but it does use menus. It has no fancy scroll lists, for example, but it can display a list of on-screen options from which users can make selections. (Who needs all that window dressing anyway? Most users just want to get the job done.)

Planning What You Want Users to Do

Ah, where to begin? Start with the old-style computer if you wish — paper and pencil (it never needs to be upgraded and works even without electricity). Then draw a picture of what you want users to see and do when they use the UNIX program you create.

Here are the steps to follow:

1. **Know what you want the program to do before you set out to design the user interface.**

2. **Pretend to be a person who will use your program.**

   Pretend that you have no information about the program except perhaps its name and a general idea of how the program should be able to help you.

3. **List on paper the menu selections you want users to be able to make when your program begins.**

4. **For each possible user selection, list what you want the computer to do when a user chooses that option.**

   For example, this following list shows the first task a user has to do; the corresponding lists contain the next set of tasks:

   1.Opening screen

   a.Locate telephone number

   Enter telephone number

   Display telephone number

   Change telephone number

   Return to preceding menu

   Exit

   b.Change entry

   Enter telephone number

   Display telephone number

   Change telephone number

   Cancel preceding change

   Return to preceding menu

   Exit

> ***c.Add new entry***
>
> *Enter new information*
>
> *Cancel new information*
>
> *Return to preceding menu*
>
> *Exit*

Don't be afraid to make a mistake (that's why they make pencil erasers). The only way you can perfect your programming skills is by trial-and-error (and maybe you'll be on *Court TV*).

The more you use paper and pencil to create a plan, the easier it is to translate your perfect set of planning notes into a full-scale UNIX program. After you finish your plan, you can concentrate on getting the computer to do what you want.

Planning What You Want the Computer to Do

A computer is supposed to do more than anyone who uses the computer. (That's to say, users are supposed to have to do little to perform a task, and computers are supposed to do most of the work!) That's the concept behind computer automation: Your program displays options on-screen and asks users to simply press the corresponding key on the keyboard for whatever task they want the computer to perform.

A computer must know what to do both before and after users of a UNIX program make menu selections from the keyboard. This list shows just some of the tasks that you, as a programmer, must consider ahead of time for any computer that runs one of your programs. Your UNIX program should be able to do the following:

1. **Run the correct shell for your program:** Because you write UNIX programs in a shell language (the C shell, for example — no seashore jokes, please), the computer must have the correct shell running so that your program can work.

2. **Do a little "housekeeping":** The computer should clear the screen of any text that's displayed so that it doesn't confuse the user of your program.

3. **Display text on-screen:** Each line of text must be displayed on-screen in the correct order. The text is a combination of labels, choices, and instructions.

4. **Take a breather:** The computer simply waits until the user presses a key on the keyboard.

5. **Decide what to do after the user presses any key.** (Don't go looking for the "any" *key* on your keyboard — there isn't one.)

6. **Determine which keyboard keys to respond to and what to do when the user presses those keys.**

7. **Ignore some keys if they aren't the valid keys the user can press to make a selection.**

8. **Decide whether to erase what's on-screen when the user presses one of the allowable keys.**

9. **Do something special:** Show other choices on-screen, for example, or find some information and display it.

10. **Remove all the text that has been placed on-screen:** Clean up your mess so that another program (or someone's mother) doesn't have to do it for you.

Designing the Screen Layout

Now it's time to decide how the screens for your programs should look: Sketch each screen you want your program to display to users.

First, come up with a title, or some words that generally describe the screen. A single line of text at the top of the screen is sufficient.

The content of the rest of the screen depends on what the computer is doing when the screen is being shown. Here are some common uses for screen displays:

- ✔ Display an appropriate message to users
- ✔ List menu options
- ✔ Provide information, such as names and addresses in a file
- ✔ Collect user information

Understand what menus do

All of us, at some point, have chosen items from menus regardless of whether those menus were part of those frustrating telephone-answering systems ("Press 1 if you want the sales department; press 2 if you want the complaint department") or were displayed on a computer screen.

Some reasons for using menus in computer programs are obvious:

- ✔ It's an easy way for users to tell a computer what they want it to do.

- ✔ Tasks are isolated so that the programmer (you) can focus on giving the computer the correct instructions necessary to carry out a task.

- ✔ Menus show only tasks that can be performed immediately. Tasks not appropriate for the current activity are not made available. For example, you can't ask a computer program to change a telephone number until you tell it to find the number in a telephone directory.

Maintain consistency

All of us are creatures of habit. We wake up at approximately the same time every day, arrive at work on schedule, have a cup of coffee, and then arrive at home like clockwork to get ready for a repeat performance the following day (some of us should also get a life!).

Each of us is generally consistent, and so are all the other people we depend on, such as spouses, the people who make our coffee, the local dry cleaner who makes sure that our clothes look sharp, and so on.

Just as people are usually consistent, so should the programs they use after arriving at their workplace. Most people like to jump right into a program and put the computer through its paces — no one usually has the time to learn how to use a program. This is only possible if the way someone uses one program is the same way as they use all the other programs.

If users have to ponder for more than a few minutes about how to use a computer program, they usually give up and decide that the program is junky (but they normally use words that I can't repeat in a family book).

How do you prevent your programs from being tossed in the garbage can? You have to make the user interface in your programs consistent with similar programs. Don't be too creative, or else you may confuse someone who is using your program for the first time.

Choose your words carefully

The words you use on-screen in your programs are critical to the design of a quality user interface. If users don't understand the terms you use, they can't use your program.

Here are some tips to make your programs communicate effectively with the people who use them:

✔ **Avoid using acronyms (words formed from the first letter of multiple-word phrases).** For example, don't tell users to "Take the EXE and send it via FTP so that your OS can take it from there."

✔ **Make sure that the words you use to describe an option reflect precisely what happens when that option is chosen.** Don't name an option Edit, for example, when Edit An Address more accurately describes what the option does.

✔ **Use simple words that are easy to understand.** Don't show off your vocabulary when you're designing a computer program.

Here's a typical opening menu for a personnel database program:

```
FOR OFFICIAL USE ONLY

Personnel database

1. Display information about an employee
2. Add information about a new employee

Q Quit

Enter your selection:
```

The first line specifies that only authorized staff members are permitted to use the program. The second line on the screen simply tells users that this is a personnel program.

The first user option, "Display information about an employee," starts the user down the path toward locating and changing information about an employee. The screen that's displayed if users choose this option displays the employee information and asks whether they want to edit the information or delete the employee's name from the database, as shown here:

```
Confidential Personnel Information

Bob Smith        Social Security #.: 555-55-5555
555 Any Street    Title: Office Manager
Anywhere, USA 55555  Start Date: 1/2/89

Department: Administration    Salary: $75,000

  1. Edit information
  2. Delete information
  Q Quit

Enter your selection:
```

The second option from the original example, "Add information about a new
employee," sends users down a different path, on which they can enter into the
database some information about a new employee.

The last user option is the escape hatch: If users don't want to continue with
the program, they can just press Q to quit the program.

Finally, there is a single line of instruction that tells the user to make a selection.

Keep your menu tree pruned

Don't you hate having to spend more time choosing items from menus than you
do using a program? Now you have an opportunity to fix that problem in the programs that you create by minimizing your program's *menu tree,* or list of menus.

No magic number exists for the number of menus you should put in a program.
You should use just a few menus and then ask a friend to test your program. If
that person gets discouraged trying to navigate through your menus, you know
that you have used too many. Take out your tree pruner and trim some of the
branches on your menu tree.

Because someone who uses your UNIX program wants to do something other than just respond to your perfectly designed menus, each menu should address all possible tasks a user may want to accomplish. After your program finds an address and displays it on-screen, for example, a user can modify the address, delete the address from the file, return to the preceding menu, or just leave your program.

If users decide to modify the information that's displayed, you don't have to ask which piece of information they want to edit — it's obvious. A better idea is to enable *the user* to change the information.

As you plan your UNIX program menus, keep in mind all the times you have had to step your way through one of those telephone menus (for example "Press 1 if you want to shoot the person who designed this system"). You're the program-mer who will make someone happy or mad by making your menus easier to use than those telephone menus.

Remember that flexibility lowers frustration

The best type of program is one that works the way the user works. Because each user works a little differently from every other user, your UNIX programs must be flexible so that they don't cramp anyone's style. This task is *not* an easy one. Try putting yourself in the place of someone who will use your program, and then ask these questions:

- ✔ Am I backtracking through the menus too much?
- ✔ Does this program flow naturally?
- ✔ Can I move quickly from one task to another?

If you find yourself having a problem using your program, you can expect that someone who uses your program will also have the same problem. Make sure that any problem is resolved and that your program works effortlessly.

Avoid dead ends

A good program enables users to move around the program quickly without having to retrace their steps. Nothing is more frustrating than to follow a long menu trail only to discover that you ended up in the wrong place. The only way out is to turn around and follow the trail back to where you started.

You can avoid these dead ends by always enabling users to jump to key posi-tions in your program (you're giving users the chance to say, "Beam me home, Scotty"). Decide which menus in your program are the important ones (the ones that start the program or perform another major task, such as display the screen used to locate information), and then include these on other menus in your program so that users can jump to them quickly.

Always make sure that each menu contains an option for exiting the program. This option is an escape hatch, in case a user panics and wants to stop using your program.

Let your program be the teacher

Few computer users ever take the time to read the documentation that comes with their programs. Most people just start a program right up, confident that they can zip through the screens in a flash. They apparently believe that any program that requires reading those manuals just isn't worth owning. However, not all the features of a program are obvious — some require the user to read the instruction manual or go to class to fully utilize the features of the program.

If this sounds all too familiar to you, you're in the majority. As a programmer, you must deal with the problem of knowing that few users will read any documentation you write to show them how to use your program. Without reading the documentation, chances are users will not be able to use your program.

Here are a few ways to handle this situation:

- ✔ Make sure that you provide clear on-screen instructions whenever you expect a user to respond to your program.

- ✔ Include a single line of text to describe what a user should do next.

- ✔ Provide detailed instructions on a Help screen that users can display by pressing the Help option on any menu in your program.

- ✔ Always define on the Help screen any technical term you use in the program.

Chapter 3
Writing Your First UNIX Program

● ●

In This Chapter

▶ Outlining your program

▶ Choosing a shell language to use

▶ Choosing a text editor

▶ Writing UNIX code for your program

● ●

*T*o have your computer do something, you must state each thing that you want it to do. Computers always do what they are told to do. So if you give your computer instructions that are unclear or out of order, your computer will follow those directions without question.

Before you can speak the language of programmers (*nerdish,* it's sometimes called), you need to learn programming etiquette.

  ✔ A single instruction to your computer is called a *command.*

  ✔ Several commands together are called *code.*

  ✔ All the instructions that are needed to complete the task are called a *program.*

According to programming etiquette, programmers never write a program. They write code. And only uncool programmers would ask to see your series of commands. "Let me see your code" is the proper way to ask permission to snoop into someone else's program. (But who asks before taking a peek?)

Before You Write a UNIX Program

You have to write instructions in a language that your computer understands, otherwise your computer won't do anything. Before you write an instruction, you must choose a computer language. When using UNIX, the language is a shell language. A *shell language* has special commands called *reserved words.* These are words that have a special meaning to UNIX, so you must be careful whenever they are used in your program. Here are a few:

case	else	set
clear	foreach	sentenv
continue	if	then
echo	read	while

UNIX code is a bunch of shell language reserved words joined together to form a program. When your computer reads a reserved word, it says to itself, "I remember how to do that." This is just like your dog that knows what to do when you say "Sit." (That is, if your dog is well trained! My dog just sits there ignoring me, but at least my computer follows my commands.)

Your UNIX program can be one reserved word or hundreds of reserved words strung together. One-word programs usually perform one task. For example, a program that has the command ls — which is short for "list" — displays the current directory on the screen . . . and does nothing else. Longer programs can do many things.

No one in their right mind would write one long program that contains hundreds and hundreds of reserved words. Your computer wouldn't have trouble reading all those words, but you would become so confused that changing the program or finding an error in it would be unmanageable.

Outline your program

If you were going to build your dream house, you wouldn't start by hammering lumber together. Instead you'd sit down with your paper and pencil to sketch out your ideas.

When you want to write a UNIX program, follow the same procedure for building your dream house. Sit down and write in English (or another language, if you prefer) all the steps that your computer must do to complete the task.

As you compose your outline, you write a mixture of our everyday language with reserved words. This combination is called *pseudo code*. Your outline may have an element that reads something like this: "If the letter Q is pressed, then end the program." The words if and then are reserved words, but the other words are not. Don't worry; you'll soon learn to distinguish reserved words from everything else. Here's a typical example of pseudo code that shows you how reserved words get mixed with regular language when you outline your program. I put the reserved words in bold so that you can pick them out. (Don't worry about the indentation yet; that's just for readability.) The program is something that is probably familiar to you if you have ever started a program that first asked you to enter your user identification and a special password. This outline shows all the steps that your computer must take to check your identification:

1. Start the C shell

2. Clear the screen

3. Show the title

4. Tell the user to enter a user ID

5. Wait for the user to enter a user ID

6. Save the user ID in memory

7. Tell the user to enter a password

8. Don't display the password on the screen

9. Wait for the user to enter a password

10. Compare the user ID with known user IDs

11. **if** the user ID is found **then**

12.   Compare the password with the user ID's password

13. **if** the password matches **then**

14.   Show the opening menu

15. **else**

16.   Tell the user the wrong password was entered

17.   Clear the screen

18.   End the program

19. **endif**

20. **else**

21.   Tell the user the wrong user ID was entered

22.   Clear the screen

23.   End the program

24. **endif**

Be logical

Each line in your program plan must be in the order in which you want the computer to do the task. Think of how you would do what you want the computer to do. Write down those steps on your paper.

For example, here are the steps needed to ask someone to enter a menu choice at the keyboard:

1. Clear the screen of any text.
2. Show the menu on the screen.
3. Tell the user to enter the letter that corresponds to the desired menu option.
4. Wait for keyboard input.

Just think what the computer would do if you told it to show the menu on the screen and then to clear the screen of any text (unless you want to elicit the reaction "There's something wrong with my monitor!" from your users).

Most errors in your program, which are called *bugs,* occur because the computer follows an instruction that is out of the proper order. (See Chapter 18 for information on bugs and debugging.) Instructions that are out of order are the hardest errors to find, especially if your program has hundreds of lines of code.

Keep track of loose ends

Your plan for your program can easily become confusing, especially if you want your computer to do a lot of stuff. Even a very simple task for you to perform takes a lot of instructions for the computer to follow.

A basic thing such as checking your user ID and password takes 24 lines in UNIX code. Imagine how many lines you would require for even the simplest program that you have in mind.

Here are a few ways to avoid losing your way through your plan:

- ✔ Place each instruction on its own line in your plan.
- ✔ Assign numbers to each line.
- ✔ Indent instructions that are associated with the previous instruction (such as when the if reserved word is used).

Break down large programs into parts

Before you actually write a program, I want to steer you toward some good programming habits. You can make your large program easier to work with by breaking it down into several smaller programs. After each of these small programs is completed, you can call each one from other programs as they are needed.

Each small program that is part of a larger program is called a *subprogram*. (In other computer languages, these subprograms are known as functions, procedures, and subroutines.) A subprogram contains all the reserved words necessary to perform one particular task. Each time you want your computer to do this task, you call the subprogram.

One subprogram may instruct the computer to display a menu on the screen. Another subprogram may tell the computer to read what someone entered at the keyboard and compare it with menu options. But not every program needs to have subprograms. If you don't have problems reading the code in your program, you probably don't need to create subprograms. I explain more about subprograms in Chapter 14.

Find repeated code

Don't be surprised if your plan for your program grows rapidly. It's like sketching the layout of your new home, and then adding a formal dining room, a formal living room, and the family dining room, and an informal living room . . .

At some point you must sit back and ask yourself if you really need all this in your house. Then you review the plans for economy. Is there anything duplicated in the plans? Can one thing be used for another purpose? Do you really need a water fountain in the doghouse?

Here is a way to reduce the size of your program:

1. **Look for instructions that are repeated in your plans.**

   For example, how many times does the computer display the same menu?

2. **Place instructions that are repeated into a subprogram, and then plan to have your computer call the subprogram each time it is needed.**

   See Chapter 14 for more on subprograms.

3. **Give the subprogram a name that reflects the task that it performs.**

   For example, *openingmenu* is a good name for the subprogram that displays the opening menu. (Did anyone really go to MIT for that?)

Dividing your program into subprograms helps a lot when you make changes to the program. For example, say that in five places in your program you have the computer display the opening menu. If you modify the opening menu, you have to make those changes in five places. But if the opening menu is a subprogram, you make only one change.

Test your newfound knowledge

1. What are reserved words?

    a. Words used by shy people

    b. Special instructions that every programming language has

    c. Words to get you into an expensive restaurant

    d. Orders given to reservist in the Army

2. How can you design a large program without getting lost?

    a. Have a team of programmers write your program for you.

    b. Copy someone else's idea.

    c. You would never attempt such a project.

    d. Outline your program before writing UNIX code.

Translate Your Program into UNIX Code

After you have spent days fine tuning your plan for your UNIX program, you can turn your attention to translating your plan into UNIX code. Don't rush into writing code. Many programmers make this common mistake. You'll have plenty of time to write your program.

Concentrate on following the logic of your plan. Keep an eye peeled for wrong turns and the correct instruction being given at the wrong time. Even the best programmers make mistakes in logic.

You'll find it easier to track down those bugs in your plan before you begin building your program. It's like finding out that the doorway in the plans for your dream house is too small before the contractor begins building the front of your house.

Outline — line by line

Begin translating your program plan into UNIX code a line at a time. Each line of your plan eventually becomes one or more lines of the program. It all depends on the task that you want your computer to perform. Some tasks can be performed with one reserved word; others require several reserved words.

Understanding what UNIX code can do

You can have your computer do all sorts of things by giving it the correct instructions. And the instructions that you give the computer are written in UNIX code. You can use UNIX code to have your computer do the following, for example:

- Calculate a result

- Show the result on the screen

- Store information in a file

- Retrieve information from a file

- Read characters from the keyboard

If you want to calculate the number of stocks that you have that are worth the money you paid for them, a UNIX program can perform the calculation. You must provide necessary information, of course.

After your computer completes the calculations, you probably want to display the results on the screen. To do this, you need to use the echo reserved word followed by the results of the calculation.

You could enter the number of stocks directly into your program. This is called *hard coded* and should generally be avoided because you would have to change the program each time a value changes (what a waste of time!). Another way is to have your program ask you to enter each stock price.

Either way, the result of the calculation is typically stored in a part of your computer's memory that is identified by a name that you give it. This is called a *variable*. Whenever you want the computer to use the result, you use the name of the variable preceded by a dollar sign ($). (I explain variables in Chapter 4.)

Here the computer is told to display on the screen the value contained in the memory location called BestStocks. BestStocks is the name of the variable:

```
echo $BestStocks
```

Of course, your UNIX program can do a lot more than turn your computer into the world's most expensive calculator.

Nearly anything that you can imagine (except finding you a rich spouse) can be performed by your computer if you give your computer the proper shell language instructions.

Don't worry about the UNIX jargon yet, but I want to give you an example. Here is what you need to do if you want to translate your outline into UNIX code. In any case, your outline should look something like the following:

1. Start the C shell.

2. Clear the screen.

3. Show the title.

4. Ask the user to enter his or her first name.

5. Wait for the user to enter the name.

6. Display a hello message using the user's name.

7. End the program.

Make note of the reserved words that you use in your outline. Avoid guessing. Feel free to look up the reserved words in any book. (I love an open book test, don't you?)

By the way, many programmers use an editor instead of paper and pencil. An *editor* is a simple word processor, and I talk about editors later in this chapter.

Make your outline correspond to UNIX code

Now number each part of your UNIX program to correspond to the line numbers on your program plan as you write your code. These numbers help you make sure that you don't skip a part of the program. But don't think that you have to know this code now. This is just an example of how your code would look as you translate your outline into UNIX code. It seems like step seven is missing. This step ends the program. However, you don't need to tell the computer when to end the program. It knows to stop when there are no more instructions.

```
1. #!/bin/csh
2. clear
3. echo "Welcome To My First UNIX Program"
4. echo "Enter your first name: "
5. set response = $<
6. echo "Hello, $response"
```

Remove the numbers from your program when you are ready to run the program. (UNIX programs do not use line numbers.)

The following sample shows you what your program would look like, ready to run!

```
#!/bin/csh
clear
echo "Welcome To My First UNIX Program"
echo "Enter your first name: "
set response = $<
echo "Hello, $response "
```

Don't become upset if you find yourself unable to translate your program outline line by line into your program like the example I used. Just like translating English to Spanish, such a translation is not always so direct.

The sample program has reserved words that are confusing. You learn about them throughout this book, but I want to give a brief explanation here just in case you can't wait.

- ✔ The `#!/bin/csh` tells your computer to start the C shell.
- ✔ The `clear` reserved word clears the screen.
- ✔ The `echo` reserved word tells the computer to show the text.
- ✔ The symbols `$<` take the characters someone enters at the keyboard and save them in your computer's memory in a location called `response`.
- ✔ The dollar sign ($) is used in front of the word response to display on the screen the characters that are stored at that memory location.

So will that keep you happy for now?

Choose a UNIX Shell

A *shell* is the program that sits between you and the UNIX kernel. The *kernel* is the program that talks to your computer. The shell program reads your instructions, translates those instructions into something that your computer understands, and sends the translated instructions to your computer.

There are many shell programs. Each one might speak a different language. This can be a problem for you. The shell program that runs your program may not be the shell program that is on the computer of the person who uses your program.

You hope that many people are going to use your program. (How else can you become rich?) So, how are you sure that all of them will be running the shell program that you use? You can't. But you can maximize your chances of exposure if you follow some basic guidelines and are familiar with what a shell can do. I explain a little about each of the three main shells next.

The Bourne shell

Back in 1979, Stephen Bourne created the first major shell program for UNIX. And guess what he called it? The Bourne shell, of course! Nearly every copy of UNIX comes with the Bourne shell.

You start the Bourne shell by typing `sh` into your computer at the command line; then press the Enter key.

The C shell

Well, just when Bourne thought he'd built the invention of the century, along came some guy with a better idea — Bill Joy from the University of California at Berkeley. He's the guy who came up with the idea for the C shell. Joy capitalized on the weaknesses in the Bourne shell. The C shell used reserved words that are used in the C programming language (the language that some programmers love and the rest of us can live without).

Bourne shell programs couldn't run in the background. They always had to take control of the screen and keyboard. You couldn't just tell your computer to go do something and come back when it was finished. Joy's C shell could do this and soon became the shell program of choice on many computers running UNIX.

Start the C shell by typing csh and then pressing the Enter key.

The Korn shell

Just when Joy seemed to be on the top of the heap, along came David Korn, one of those whiz kids at Bell Labs. He created a shell that overcame the weaknesses of the C shell. The Korn shell could run Bourne shell scripts without changing the script. And newer versions of the Korn shell offer windowing capabilities. However, the Korn shell is not found on every computer that runs UNIX.

Start the Korn shell by typing ksh and then pressing the Enter key.

Consider Your Shell Options

The difficulty in picking the UNIX shell to use for your program is unique to UNIX. You don't have this problem when you write a program for DOS and Windows machines, or for the Mac. In each case, Bill Gates or the guys at Apple Computers decide for you which shell is used.

Here are a few points to consider when choosing a shell language:

- Anticipate who will be using your program.

    If the program is going to run only on your computer, whatever shell you pick is fine.

- Decide how someone is going to use your program.

    If your program is supposed go off and do something in the background while you do something else (such as copying a large file), the C shell and Korn shell are good candidates.

✔ Look for the common shell that will be on the computers running your program.

If you're writing your program for a bunch of friends who are using a fancy new shell program that hit the Internet, you, too, should use that shell program.

My Choice for a UNIX Shell

Let's cut to the chase. My choice for the shell program to use for your UNIX programs is the C shell. Some programmers will disagree, but here's why I made this pick.

The C shell is more flexible than the Bourne shell and is available on nearly all the computers that will be running your program. C shell programs can also be read by the Korn shell.

Most versions of the C shell are supported by the suppliers of the UNIX operating system. This means that if you run into trouble, you have someone to call (even if you have to pay a support fee).

Consider Your Editor Options

You must eventually write your program in an electronic form and save it to a file. Although there is nothing stopping you from using a word processor to write your program, most UNIX programmers prefer to use a special kind of word processor called a *text editor*. A text editor is a plain Jane when it comes to word processing. You won't find any fancy features in it.

A number of text editors are available in UNIX that you can use to create your program. (Isn't anything simple in UNIX?) Each editor has its fans and detractors.

Choose an editor

The choice of which text editor to use depends on how simple and powerful you want this tool to be. And, probably more important, your choice may depend on which text editor is available on your computer.

✔ The old standby is ed. This text editor lets you write or change a line of a program one line at a time. Because ed isn't a full-screen text editor, most programmers simply skip over this choice.

✔ Another old standby is vi. You can find vi on most computers that run UNIX. This is a full-screen text editor — that's to say, you can work on one screen at a time instead of line by line. But vi is a little tricky to use. (Was it the letter k that moved the cursor to the right?)

✔ A more powerful text editor is emacs. This text editor is available on some computers and can work on several files at the same time.

And the envelope please. The winner for the text editor that I use in *UNIX Programming For Dummies* is vi! I make this selection only because vi is the full-screen text editor that you most likely have on your computer. And guess what? Even though I explain a little bit about vi in the next sections, I also include more details in Appendix B.

Give vi *a try*

At the command line, type **vi** into your computer and press the Enter key. A full screen of tildes (~) will be displayed. Each *tilde* is a blank line in your program. You move around your program by performing keyboard gymnastics with your fingers. Don't bother trying the arrow keys, they won't work.

vi has three modes that you need to know about:

✔ *Command mode* allows you to move about your program without changing the text itself — you just enter commands. You are in the command mode when you first start vi. You can tell vi to enter the command mode at any time by pressing the Esc key.

✔ *Insert mode* allows you to enter or edit text. From the command mode, press the letter i or letter a to enter the insert mode. After choosing the insert mode with the letter i, you can insert text before the cursor. With the letter a, you add text after the cursor.

✔ *Last line mode* is used to save your program; load another program; or quit vi. Press the Esc key to enter the command mode (unless you are already in it) and then press the colon (:) followed by the last line command that you want.

Many programmers find vi a little awkward to use, especially when much better text editors are available for DOS, Windows, and the Mac. After you become used to working with vi, however, you won't give it a second thought. It's like driving with a stick shift. After you drive with a stick shift for a while, it becomes easy. (See Table 3-1 for a summary of the most useful commands in vi.)

Table 3-1	v i **Commands**

Note: You must be in the command mode to use these commands — and keep in mind that UNIX is case sensitive, so type the command as I give it.

Command	*What It Does*
Moving the cursor	
j	Down one line
k	Up one line
h	Left one character
l	Right one character
$	To the end of the current line
0	To the beginning of the current line
+	To the beginning of the next line
-	To the beginning of the preceding line
Deleting	
dd	Entire line
x	Character under the cursor
X	Character to the left of the cursor
5dd	Delete the current line plus the next four lines
Undeleting	
u	Last change
U	All changes to the line
Inserting text	
i	In front of the cursor
I	At the beginning of the line
a	After the cursor
A	At the end of the current line
Copying and pasting text	
yy	Copies line to the computer's memory
p	Pastes text from the computer's memory to the screen after cursor

(continued)

Table 3-1 *(continued)*

Command	What It Does
Scrolling the screen	
Ctrl+F	Forward one screen
Ctrl+B	Back one screen
Ending vi and saving changes	
ZZ	Quits vi and saves changes
:w	Saves changes without exiting vi
:q	Quits vi
:q!	Quits vi without saving changes
Changing modes	
i	From command mode to insert mode
a	From command mode to insert mode (append)
:	From command mode to last line mode
Searching text	
/*text*	Searches from cursor to end of file for text you indicate
/	Repeats preceding search
?	Repeats preceding search from cursor to beginning of file
:*n*	Finds line number in which *n* is the line number you want to locate

Avoid common vi *mistakes*

Whenever you use an unfamiliar text editor, you are bound to make a few errors. You'll be joining the ranks of many professional programmers when you are tripped up by some of vi's common traps. Here are a few that anyone can make:

- ✔ You forget about the vi modes.

  When vi shows you an empty page, you begin typing. Only a portion of what you type appears on the page. You were not in the insert mode . . . until you inadvertently typed the letter i in your text. From that point forward you were inserting text — but not before.

✔ You try to move to a blank line.

Because `vi` fills the page with tildes (~) to symbolize a blank line, you assume that you can move the cursor anywhere on the page (You don't have this trouble with Microsoft Word, do you?). Blank lines are not really there. You must open each line by pressing the Enter key or using the `o` key in the command mode.

✔ You forget to specify a name for the file when you start `vi`.

This happens all the time when you are in a rush to write your program. The solution is to name the file when you write using the last line mode (substituting the name of the file for `filename`):

```
:w filename
```

You can bet that you'll soon find your *own* common mistakes. But as long as you try not to repeat them, you'll do all right.

Stopping `vi` and saving changes

It's easy to start `vi` and enter text on the page. Getting out of `vi` is a little tricky. You can eject yourself from `vi` in several ways when you are in command mode:

✔ Type `:q` to stop `vi`.

If you haven't saved your file, `vi` prompts you to do so.

✔ Type `ZZ` to save your changes and to stop `vi`.

✔ Type `::wq` to save your changes and to stop `vi`.

✔ Type `:q!` to stop `vi` without saving your changes.

Write Your First UNIX Program

Now it's time for you to sit down in front of your computer and write your first UNIX program. Begin with a simple menu program. The program displays a list of things that the user can do with your program. The program also reads the selection the user makes on the keyboard. Later in this book, you can build on this program and have your program do something when someone chooses an option.

Write a program to display a menu

The purpose of this program is to display a simple menu on the screen. For this example, you are going to make a telephone book menu that looks like this when your program runs:

```
The Telephone Book

1. Display A Telephone Number
2. Add A New Telephone Number

Q Quit

Enter your selection:
```

Here's what to do:

1. Type `vi mymenu`

This starts `vi` and names your program *mymenu*.

2. Type `i` **when the blank page appears on the screen.**

This command takes you to the insert mode.

If you choose to use another text editor besides `vi`, you wouldn't start the text editor with the commands shown here. You probably can find how to use the text editor by typing `man <text editor name>`. (Of course, use the name of your text editor instead of typing <text editor name>. For example, if you are using `emacs`, type `man emacs`.) The manual pages should appear on your screen. If they don't, the manual pages are not on your computer. Call the person who is responsible for your computer and ask that these pages be installed.

3. Type the UNIX code that follows:

```
#!/bin/csh
clear
echo " "
echo "The Telephone Book "
echo " "
echo "1. Display A Telephone Number "
echo "2. Add A New Telephone Number "
echo " "
echo "Q Quit "
echo " "
echo "Enter your selection: "
```

Here is what you are doing!

You are starting the C shell script by using `#!/bin/csh` as the first command of your program.

Next, you are using the `clear` reserved word to have your computer erase any text that might already be displayed on the screen.

You are then using the `echo` reserved word to display text as well as blank lines on the screen. All the characters between the quotation marks are displayed.

Of course, you don't need to copy this program exactly. Become a little adventurous and experiment. Change the text, change the spacing, go a little crazy. This is the only way that you will really learn how to create a UNIX program.

Save your program

After you are satisfied that all the instructions in your program are in the correct order and the proper words are used to tell the computer what to do, you are ready to save your file.

Here are several ways to save your file using the `vi` text editor (and some are familiar to you if you read the earlier section "Stopping `vi` and saving changes").

- ✔ `ZZ`: Saves your file and exits `vi`
- ✔ `:w`: Saves your file without exiting `vi`
- ✔ `:wq`: Saves your file and exits `vi`
- ✔ `:w filename`: Saves your file under a new name that you specify (so `:w mymenu2`: saves your file as *mymenu2*).

Always save your program while you are still writing your program in `vi`. Until your program is saved in a file, everything you type only exists in your computer's memory. If you turn off your computer (or the power company does it for you), you lose all your hard work!

Make your program work

Your program is almost ready to run, but not just yet. You still have to tell your computer that your file is an executable file. An *executable file* is a file that contains instructions for your computer to follow.

Here's how this is done:

1. **Move to the directory that contains your file if you are not already in that directory. Just type**

   ```
   cd /mydirectory
   ```

   Remember, replace mydirectory with the directory name on your computer that contains your program file.

2. **Make the file an executable file by using the** chmod **utility:**

   ```
   chmod 711 mymenu
   ```

   This command allows everyone to run your program called *mymenu* — but only you can see the file itself. (Refer to Chapter 1 where I explain a little about the chmod utility.)

3. **You can run your program by typing the name of the program at the command line and pressing Enter like this:**

   ```
   mymenu
   ```

   The program displays the menu on the screen and prompts you to enter a selection from the menu. After you enter your selection, the program ends.

Making changes to your program

Change your program at any time by recalling your program to the screen using the vi text editor or the text editor of your choice.

For example, using vi as my model, I simply type vi mymenu at the command prompt. Here I can start vi again and use the name of the program file. Remember that when you start vi, you're in the command mode.

Expect to edit your programs frequently. Always make another copy of your program under a different name before you begin changing your program. You can use this backup copy of your program in case you destroy your program during editing.

Part II
The Basics of Writing Code

WELL HOT DANG!! FINALLY–A FAULT TOLERANT PRETZEL MAKER THAT RUNS UNDER UNIX !

LARRY'S HOMEMADE PRETZELS

LARRY'S HOME MADE PRETZELS

In this part . . .

*G*reat! You've reached the point when you actually start writing UNIX code to make your computer do something worthwhile. So far, you've learned the finer points of building a user interface (with an occasional UNIX command sprinkled about).

What matters to those who use your program is what your program can do for them. Just because you designed the perfect plan for your program doesn't mean that your work is finished.

Writing instructions for a computer can intimidate even the hearty adventurer, but there is nothing to fear. Writing UNIX code is as simple as giving someone step-by-step instructions. This you've done most of your life.

Caution: programming is addicting and a whole lot of fun once you get started. So don't waste any more time. Learn to code.

Chapter 4

Using Variables

*W*hen you know what you want your computer to do, the time is right to write UNIX code. The place you begin to write your UNIX code is in a text editor file (as I explain in Chapter 3).

Your text editor file that contains your program just tells your computer to do something. The simplest program that you can write tells your computer to stop running your program. Only the reserved word exit is used in the program, as shown here:

```
exit
```

You want your programs to do more than this task, however. For example, you can design a program to ask someone for a name and address. You also need to write instructions into your program to tell the computer to read this information and do something with it.

Reading Data

Information that your program receives from someone who uses it is called *data* — now you also know where the character on *Star Trek: The Next Generation* got its name. Good programs follow three simple steps:

  ✔ They get data from the keyboard or a file.

  ✔ They do something with the data.

  ✔ They show the data on the screen or in a report.

The reason for writing your program is to turn your computer into an electronic factory. In one end goes all the data that is needed to do something. And out the other end comes useful information. This is all that a word processor, a spreadsheet, and a database program actually do. And the data used by all these programs manipulates two things: strings and numbers.

Strings

A *string* is usually a bunch of letters or characters that are strung together. A character can be a hyphen or any character that you find on the keyboard. A string can be a *single* letter or character, too. A whole sentence can be a string. And this whole chapter can be a string. Any group of letters, spaces — and even numbers — can be a string (as you see later in this chapter).

Numbers

A *number* can be any number such as money, age, height, the number of friends who come over to your cookout (and don't invite you to their cookout), and so on. This category includes positive and negative numbers, as well as whole or fractional numbers.

And numbers are also characters! This behavior may be a little confusing to you, but it isn't so confusing to your computer. If you tell the computer that the number is part of an address or telephone number, the computer treats the number like a letter or character. However, if you tell the computer to add (or perform any mathematical operation) using numbers, the computer treats the numbers as numbers (not characters).

A Gentle Introduction to Variables and Values

It seems like magic that your computer knows how to keep track of the numbers and strings that someone enters into your program. Knowing that 555-55-5555 is someone's Social Security number is easy for you. Your computer just knows it as a number or a string.

Your program must tell your computer: "When someone enters 555-55-5555, give this number the name SSNum and then put it someplace. Don't forget where you put it. I'll call for it later."

Your program must also tell your computer when it needs to use the Social Security number: "Time for the Social Security number. You remember where you put it. It is under the variable name SSNum."

Your program then finds the variable SSNum and copies the number so your program can do something with it.

A *variable* is said to hold a *value*. The Social Security number that is given the variable name SSNum is a value. (In fact, it's the key to all of your financial, medical, and employment history!)

Variables 101

UNIX has two kinds of variables:

- Those you create that only your program uses: local variables
- Those that you or someone else creates that your program and other programs can use: environment variables

When your program needs to save data, you create (or *declare*) what is called a *local variable*. Only your program can use this variable.

Every time you log into UNIX, a whole bunch of variables are already available. These are called *environment variables*. Environment variables contain information that tells your computer information about you and about the computer. For example, a common environment variable is EDITOR. The value that is assigned to this variable is the name of the text editor that is on your computer.

Declaring variables

You can create a variable by using the reserved words set and setenv followed by the variable name. Here's an example:

```
set firstName
setenv EDITOR vi
```

In this example, you can see the two kinds of variable being created:

- set declares a local variable (in this case, a local string variable)
- setenv declares an environment variable

Placing variables

There is no special place in your UNIX program to declare a variable. A variable can be declared anywhere in your program. However, placing a variable just anywhere isn't considered a good programming practice. Chances are that you will be hunting for those variables the next time you read your program.

A preferred programming practice is to declare all the variables at the beginning of your program. They'll all be in the same place when you need to find them.

Combining your variables

Variables of the same kind (such as two string variables) can be declared on the same line at the beginning of your program. Here's how it's done:

```
set FirstName, LastName
```

You can type as many variable names as can fit on the line. Notice that each is separated by a comma and then a space.

See how easy it can be to locate the variables that are used in your program? You don't have to search every line of the program. Simply look at the first few lines of your program to examine all the variables.

Naming variables

A variable can be called anything (and you can store anything imaginable in it). However, it just doesn't make too much sense to name a variable SSNum and then shove some telephone number in it.

Make programming UNIX easy for yourself: Give names to your variables that tell someone (like you) what kind of data is stuffed in them. Naming a variable SSNum seems right only if you intend to place a Social Security number in the variable — just like a variable called FirstName should hold the characters that are in someone's first name.

Here are some rules to follow when you name your variables. All variable names must

- ✔ Begin with a letter
- ✔ Be composed of only letters (upper or lowercase), numbers, and the underscore character (_)
- ✔ Have no spaces

Of course, a variable can't be a reserved word.

UNIX will have no problem if you follow the rules when naming variables. (Although there just may be other parts of your program that it doesn't like!) Here are some variable names that will make UNIX happy:

    DeptNo

    Fax_Num

    Acct573

Here are some variable names that will make UNIX choke:

    First Name (spaces are not allowed)

    573Acct (the first character must be a letter)

    exit (reserved words are not allowed)

Test your newfound knowledge

1. What does the following UNIX command do?

    set street, city, state, zip

    a. Words shouted by the quarterback before the ball is hiked

    b. Declares four variables

    c. Tells the computer where the user set lives

    d. Stuffs set's address into variables

2. What is the purpose for declaring variables?

    a. So you can keep your data secret from hackers

    b. To add a touch of royalty to your program: I declare you a variable

    c. To tell the computer to reserve space to store a certain type of data

    d. To make your program look complicated so you can impress your friends

Assigning numbers to variables

After you create a variable by naming it, you probably want to stuff something into the variable. This action is called *assigning a value* to the variable.

To assign a value to a variable, you must use a super-complex, scientific gizmo that requires that you have at least a masters degree in computer science from MIT (just joking). All you need to know is how to use the equal (=) sign.

Here's how you stuff a value into a numeric variable called MySalary. Instead of yelling at your computer, "Put the number 1 million in my salary variable," you just write:

```
@ MySalary = 1000000
```

You use the @ sign followed by a space and then by the numeric variable. After a space, an equal sign, and another space, you type in the value. The @ sign is a built-in function that allows you to evaluate a numeric expression — in this case, the assignment of 1000000 to the variable MySalary.

A variable can have only one value. You can change this value by assigning another value to the variable. Your computer then throws out the old value and replaces it with the new value. The old value is lost forever.

Imagine that you want to write a program that tells your computer to give you a starting salary of a million dollars. And just because you've done such a good job writing this program, you tell your computer to double your salary.

Try this one on your boss:

```
@ MySalary = 1000000
@ MySalary = 2000000
```

As your computer is reading your program, it's saying: "Let's see, you want me to create a numeric variable MySalary. I can do that. And you want me to put the number one million into this variable. I can do that too. Then you want me to erase the one million and put the number two million in its place. That doesn't make much sense, but I can do that."

Assigning strings to variables

Assigning strings to variables is just as easy as it is to stuff numbers into a variable. Here are a few differences:

⯈ `set` or `setenv` is used.

⯈ Quotation marks must surround the string to tell your computer where the string begins and ends.

⯈ A dollar sign ($) must precede a string variable whenever you refer to the variable in your program.

Now you can assign someone's first name to a string variable:

```
set FirstName = "Mary"
```

Or you can assign someone's first and last name to a string variable:

```
set Name = "Mary Smith"
```

Or assign a whole bunch of words to a string variable:

```
set MyGoal = "Buy out Bill Gates"
```

Sometimes strings consist of numbers instead of letters, but they are still strings, such as in a telephone number:

```
set Telephone = "555-5555"
```

But if you were to try this without the quotation marks . . .

```
set Telephone = 555-5555
```

Ouch! Your computer would complain. When you declared the variable, you told the computer that you wanted to store a string. In the next line you said subtract 5555 from 555 and put the difference in the string variable Telephone. But the difference is a numeric value, not a string.

Don't forget this rule: Put quotation marks around a string value.

Assigning variables to other variables

You can take data stuffed into one variable and copy it to another variable. You end up with two copies of the data. Your computer doesn't remove the data from the original variable.

Here's how you do this with a string variable:

```
set MyGoal = "Buy out Bill Gates"
set OurGoal = $MyGoal
```

Your computer is told to go to the variable MyGoal and copy the data that's there. Next, your computer is told to take that data and place it into the variable OurGoal.

You can also do this with a numeric variable:

```
@ MySalary = 1000000
@ OurSalaries = $MySalary
```

A copy of the value of your salary is taken by your computer and stuffed into the variable OurSalaries. The value of OurSalaries is the same as your salary, 1000000. Your million dollar salary remains safe in the MySalary variable.

Using Data Types

A UNIX variable can store any number or string. Your computer can become confused (and it doesn't like being confused) if you tell it one thing and then tell it to do something completely opposite.

Say that you ask your computer to find a place to stuff someone's name (create a variable). But when the time comes to do the actual stuffing, you give it the person's salary, instead.

Your computer will turn around and say something like, "Hey, what goes on? First you tell me you want to store a string. Okay, so I go do all this work and I find the perfect spot for your string. Now you give me a number. There's no room for the number there." What is more embarrassing is if someone else's computer complains — which means that everyone who uses your program will know that you goofed.

When you declare a variable, you specify the *data type* of the variable. Some computer languages have many data to handle all sizes of numbers and strings. Don't concern yourself with these choices. UNIX has just two data types:

- ✔ Numeric data type
- ✔ String data type

Be sure to check the data type of the variable in your program before you assign it a value. You won't give your computer a reason to complain about your program.

The Scope of Variables

The scope of a variable determines who can use the variable within UNIX. There are two ways that you can tell UNIX who can access a variable: local and global.

A *local variable* can be used by the program that created the variable. This property helps you to isolate the information from anything else that is running on your computer. Here's how you declare a local variable within your program:

```
set SSNum
@ Salary = 1000000
```

But what if you want to share this information with other programs? In that case, you have to declare the variable as *global*. Any program that is running on your computer can read a global variable and change the value of the global variable.

In many computer languages, such as the C language, a global variable is created by putting it in a special place in your program file. This isn't the case when you declare a global variable in UNIX. Instead, you use the `setenv` keyword, which creates an environment variable.

Here's how you declare a global variable within your program (so do this, and the whole world will know your Social Security number):

```
setenv SSNum 555-55-5555
```

You must be very careful whenever you decide to use a global variable in your program.

- ✔ Any program running on the same computer as your program can read and change the value that is stored in the global variable.
- ✔ The last value assigned to the global variable is the one that your computer keeps. So if two programs change the value of the same global variable, one program may not work correctly.
- ✔ Finding a problem caused by a wrong value assigned to a global variable can be a nightmare. You don't know which program changed it.

Understanding String Arrays

There is a way to stuff more than one value in the same variable. This concept may seem confusing to you, but your computer will have no trouble keeping track of each of those values. Programmers call this kind of variable a *string array.* You already know what a string is if you read the first part of this chapter (Hint: one or a bunch of characters). An array is a *series* of some things. A list of towns can be called an array of towns. Information about one person can also be called an array.

Here are some tips on using string arrays:

- Only string data can be assigned to the array variable
- Place the same kind of data in a string array.

  It is better to assign Bob, Mary, and Sue to a string array than Bob, Car, and 555-5555. Bob, Mary, and Sue are all first names whereas the other data have no relationship.

- Call the string array by a name that tells everyone the kind of data that will be assigned to the array.

  FirstNames may be a good name for a string array that is stuffed with first names.

Creating and displaying a string array

You declare a string array the same way as you create a string variable — by using the `set` reserved word. However, instead of assigning one value to the variable, you assign several values to it.

Your computer is smart enough to know how to treat each of these values as individual pieces of data, so consider yourself lucky. But you have to do a few things so that your computer knows to do its task:

- Separate data by a space.
- Place the data within parentheses.
- Use quotation marks around data that contains spaces.

  If you have Bob Smith as one piece of data, you must use quotations marks as such: "Bob Smith."

Here's how you assign data to a string array (that you call `direction`) and display all the data stuffed into it:

```
set direction = (north south east west)
echo $direction
```

Picking out data from a string array

Any data assigned to a string array can be picked out and used in your program. Each data stored in a string array is called an *element*. In the preceding example, north, south, east, and west are each an element of the string array called `direction`.

Your computer numbers each element of a string array — but you don't see it. These secret numbers are called *index numbers*.

You can use these numbers to tell your computer which element of the string array that you want to use in your program because the index number is the same as the order in which the data is assigned to the string array. In the preceding example, north is the first value assigned to the string array and has the index number 1. I'll use *north* as the data I want to pick out from a string array in my example:

```
set direction = (north south east west)
echo $direction[1]
```

Notice that you position the index number after the name of the string array, and the index number is enclosed in brackets. The entire array can be displayed by using a zero as the index number:

```
set direction = (north south east west)
echo $direction[0]
```

Choosing a range of data from a string array

You can use more than one piece of data that you stuffed into a string array by giving your computer a different instruction for each data that you want to use.

For example, one instruction will display the first element of the string array, and then another instruction displays the second element, and so on. But a better way to do this is to specify a range of index numbers separated by a hyphen:

```
set direction = (north south east west)
echo $direction[1-3]

north south east
```

Chapter 5

Interacting with the User

● ●

In This Chapter

▶ Getting data from the keyboard input

▶ Displaying data that the user enters

▶ Keeping your data in a file

● ●

*T*he part of the program that the user sees — the user interface — is like window dressing for your program. It makes your program look pretty. However, a pretty user interface doesn't necessarily help someone do something with your program.

If you want your program to be more useful than a pretty picture on the screen, you need it to interact with the user. Your program must do the following to interact:

✔ Get information from the user (via the keyboard)

✔ Do something with that information

✔ Show the results of what it does on the user interface

Keyboard Input

The user interface displays messages (called *prompts*) on the screen, and these messages tell someone to press a key on the keyboard — but your program can't *force* the user to press a key. Your interface is all you have.

You can't write a pretty user interface for UNIX like you see in Macs and PCs running Windows programs (unless you learn how to program X Windows and Motif). UNIX is a plain Jane, like DOS. Expect that your program will be patiently waiting until the Enter key is pressed after each piece of information is typed in. In the meantime, all the keystrokes are being collected and stored someplace in your computer called a *keyboard buffer.* After the Enter key is pressed, your program rushes to grab all those characters entered from the keyboard and stuffs them into the variables that you created for them.

Pretty UNIX

Mr. Gates gave DOS a makeover and it came out looking like Windows. However, UNIX is still undergoing its makeover. The first improvement is allowing a user to have more than one window on the screen. For this, the user needs special software called X Windows. The next improvement is jazzing up those windows with push buttons, drop-down lists, and all those things that Windows machines and Macs have. More special software is needed. This software is called Motif. So, unless you intend to learn how to build your program to use X Windows and Motif, you have to live with a simpler program.

Reading a string

Your computer isn't too bright when it has to pick up data from the keyboard (but it would like to see *us* find the square root of 365 in less than a second). Your computer doesn't know whether a number should be treated as a character or a value that will be used in a calculation. It only finds out when *you* specify the kind of variable that will be used to store the information.

After you tell the computer the correct variable to use, you must tell it to read the characters from the keyboard. The following code shows you how to tell the computer to read characters and then stuff them into a string variable.

```
#!/bin/csh
clear
echo " "
echo "Enter Your First Name: "
set FirstName = $<
```

First, #!/bin/csh tells the computer to start the C shell before clearing (clear) the screen.

Next, the computer skips a line on the screen (echo " ") and tells the user the kind of data to enter (echo "Enter Your First Name: ").

Notice this funny pair of characters: The dollar sign ($) and the less-than sign (<) instruct your computer to take all the characters entered at the keyboard and place them in the string variable FirstName. This command only kicks in when someone presses the Enter key, however.

Reading a number

If your program needs to read a number from the keyboard, a slightly different approach must be taken. The instruction that you give your computer is the same you give to read a string. However, you use a numeric variable. The following code shows you how to tell your computer to read a numeric value from the keyboard:

```
#!/bin/csh
clear
echo " "
echo "Enter Your Age: "
@ age = $<
```

This is almost the same way as your computer reads a string from the keyboard — but not quite.

`#!/bin/csh` tells the computer to start the C shell before clearing (`clear`) the

screen.

You don't need to declare the numeric variable at the top of your program like you do with a string variable.

`echo " "` then tells the computer to skip a line before the user is asked to enter some data (`echo "Enter Your Age: "`).

The at sign (@) is used in front of the name of the variable (`age`). This tells your computer that the variable age is a numeric variable. `@ age = $<` instructs your computer to take all the data entered at the keyboard and place it in the string variable `age`.

Mixing strings and numbers from the keyboard

You can mix the kind of information that your program collects from someone. Sometimes you can ask for a numeric value; other times you can ask for a string value. Your program doesn't care.

Keep in mind that it does matter to the person using your program. You must ask for the information in a logical way. For example, someone using your program won't expect to be asked for their first name, age, and then last name. That order just doesn't make sense. First name, last name, and age is an order that seems better.

Besides using common sense when requesting information, you should also ask one question at a time. The following code illustrates how to read both string and numeric data in a logical order:

```
#!/bin/csh
clear
echo " "
echo "Enter Your First Name: "
set FirstName = $<
echo "Enter Your Last Name: "
set LastName = $<
echo "Enter Your Age: "
@ age = $<
```

The user is, of course, prompted for first name, last name, and then age.

Displaying Data that Someone Enters

Now that your program has the information that someone entered, it needs to do something with the information. The program can use the data in a calculation, store the information into a file on your disk, or do practically anything you can imagine.

The most common thing to do with the information is make it show on the screen. Another thing to do is to compare the data with information that you already have in your computer — but let's leave this second activity for now and just try a simple display.

Here are some things you should know about displaying information:

✔ Data displayed on the screen still remains in the variable. (Data is stored in a variable, and then the program copies the data from the variable to the screen. The data remains both on the screen and stored in the variable.)

This process allows the program to do something else with the data while you are looking at it. For example, your program can store a salary in the MySalary variable and then display the salary on the screen. While the salary is displayed, the program can use the salary to calculate your new salary — assuming that you received a raise in pay.

✔ Data is always displayed at the cursor on the screen. Say that your program displays this text "Salary:". The cursor — that flashing little light that signals where you are on the screen — moves to the right of the colon (:). Next, your program displays the data that contains the salary.

> ✔ Data that is displayed can be modified, but the changed data is not automatically shown. For example, your program displays the salary on the screen. The salary is also stored in the variable MySalary. Your program then proceeds to calculate the new salary, and the result is saved in the variable MySalary. However, the old salary still remains on the screen until your program displays the variable MySalary again.

There is nothing special about the data that your computer collects from the keyboard and stores in a variable. This capability is the same as if your program told the computer to assign the value to the variable.

Displaying a string

A typical UNIX program tells someone to enter a string of characters; the program then saves the characters in a variable before displaying them on the screen. You have a choice to do the following:

> ✔ Display the characters on a single line

> ✔ Display a combination of the characters with other characters on a single line

You can have the computer show just the characters that someone entered into your program by using the echo $<variable name> on a line in your program. Of course, replace <variable name> with the name of your variable.

Characters can be combined with other characters by placing them within quotations as shown in the following code. Here, the program asks users their first name and then greets them with a big hello (but no kiss and hug).

```
#!/bin/csh
clear
echo " "
echo "Enter Your First Name: "
set FirstName = $<
echo "Hello, $FirstName"
```

Although the program added the text Hello, this string could have been stored into another string variable. I do that in the next example. With the following code, the computer is told to go to the $Greeting variable and display that string before going to the $FirstName and displaying those characters.

```
#!/bin/csh
clear
set FirstName,Greeting
```

(continued)

(continued)

```
echo $Greeting = "Hello, "
echo " "
echo "Enter Your First Name: "
set FirstName = $<
echo "$Greeting $FirstName"
```

Displaying a number

Telling your computer to show a number on the screen isn't much different than telling it to display a string. All you need to remember is to be sure to have the computer save the data in a numeric variable.

Instead of using the dollar sign ($) in front of the variable, which would make it a string variable, you must use the at sign (@).

Take a look at the following code to see how to show numeric data on the screen. Remember that you don't need to declare the numeric variable at the top of a program as you do with string variables.

```
#!/bin/csh
clear
echo " "
echo "Enter Your Age: "
@ age = $<
echo "$age"
```

Displaying strings and numbers

Numeric data and string data are collected separately. However, someone who uses your program expects to see them shown together on the same line. Let's not disappoint anyone. So here's how you can show numeric data combined with string data on the same line:

```
#!/bin/csh
clear
echo " "
echo "Enter Your First Name: "
set FirstName = $<
echo "Enter Your Age: "
@ age = $<
echo "$FirstName, $age really isn't that old."
```

`echo "Enter Your First Name: "` asks someone to enter a first name and then saves it to a variable (`FirstName`).

Next, `echo "Enter Your Age: "` asks the person to enter an age. This, too, is saved — but to a different variable (`age`).

Finally, the program shows the person's first name, age, and then a comforting comment (that no one believes): `Jim, 82 really isn't that old`.

Keeping Data in a File

It is common to put data that someone enters into your file on your hard disk. A *file* is like a file drawer (but a lot better organized). Say that you want to have your date book handy — but away from prying eyes. You could build a program that collects all those special phone numbers for you and then places them in an electronic hideaway on your computer's hard disk. Then, when Friday night rolls around, you can have your program open the file and let you choose the date of your dreams. Of course, your dream date may have other plans.

Here are some reasons for saving data to a file:

- ✔ Data will always be available to your programs.
- ✔ You won't lose information unless a disaster happens to your hard disk. And we all know that could never happen. (On the other hand, where is my tape backup?)
- ✔ You can use a UNIX utility to search the file for particular information.

The way in which you organize the data that you save to a file is important, otherwise your computer has a difficult time finding it.

In Chapter 16, you explore how to create a simple database. A database is a special kind of file that is designed to hold information that you need to find fast. For now, however, I want to show you how to take the data that your program collects and stuff it in a simple file on your hard disk.

Saving data to a new file

The whiz kids at Bell Labs decided that any time your program needs to display anything using the `echo` reserved word, it uses the screen.

That's just fine for most of your programs, but you can easily change this method to display data someplace else — such as to a file. Such a process is called *redirection,* which means changing the direction of the normal flow of data.

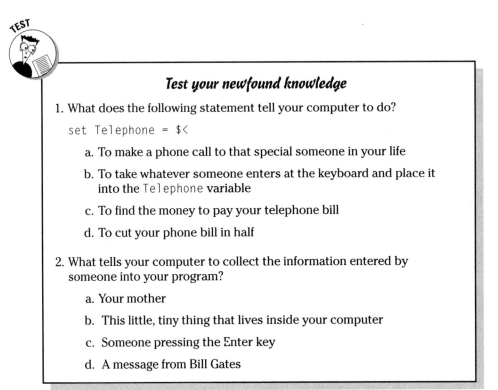

Test your newfound knowledge

1. What does the following statement tell your computer to do?

   ```
   set Telephone = $<
   ```

   a. To make a phone call to that special someone in your life

   b. To take whatever someone enters at the keyboard and place it into the Telephone variable

   c. To find the money to pay your telephone bill

   d. To cut your phone bill in half

2. What tells your computer to collect the information entered by someone into your program?

   a. Your mother

   b. This little, tiny thing that lives inside your computer

   c. Someone pressing the Enter key

   d. A message from Bill Gates

This redirection isn't hard to do at all. Take a look at the following example to see how. You've seen everything in this example before, except for something in the last line in the program.

```
#!/bin/csh
clear
echo " "
echo "Enter Your First Name: "
set FirstName = $<
echo "Enter Your Last Name: "
set LastName = $<
echo "$FirstName $LastName" > employees.dat
```

The *greater-than sign* (>)tells your computer that, instead of showing the values of the variables on the screen, it should store them in a file called employees.dat (and if I could get a peek, I could find out what's going on where you work).

Keep these points in mind:

- Your computer creates a new file when you use the greater-than sign in your program to save something to a file.

- If a file with the same name already exists, your computer will overwrite the file with the new information. The old information is lost forever, which is a long time. So be careful.

Appending data to an existing file

Who wants to overwrite information in a file every time? No one does. That's why you should use two greater-than signs (>>) instead of a single greater-than sign whenever you want to append information to the end of the file rather than overwriting the data that's already there.

The *double greater-than sign* tells your computer to add the new data at the end of the file rather than at the beginning of the file. Your computer will never overwrite and lose existing data in the file.

The following code shows practically the same program as is in the preceding example — except the new information is *appended* to the file (assuming that the file already exists!). A new file is automatically created if the file that is specified in the program does not exist.

```
#!/bin/csh
clear
echo " "
echo "Enter Your First Name: "
set FirstName = $<
echo "Enter Your Last Name: "
set LastName = $<
echo $FirstName $LastName >> employees.dat
```

Data saved to a file using the echo reserved word appears on the same line in the file just as it appears on the same line on the screen.

Displaying data that is saved to a file

The information that your computer saved to a file can be shown on the screen with the cat utility from within your program. You can tell your computer to run a utility program by entering the name of the utility in your program — just as you would type the name of the utility on the command line. This procedure is referred to as *calling a utility program*.

The inside story of redirection

Your computer needs to know where to get information. The nerds call this standard *in* (short for input). Where should your computer get data? The guys at Bell Labs answered that question when they made UNIX. Their choice was the keyboard.

Your computer also needs to know where to show information. Computer guys call this standard *out* (short for output). And where should your computer display information? The Bell Labs whiz kids decided to show it on the screen (and for this they went to MIT).

There's one more thing your computer needs to know. When something goes wrong, where do you want the error message sent?

How about the screen (brilliant)? This standard is called *error*.

You can change how information flows in your computer by using the redirection signs: the less-than (<) and greater-than (>) signs.

- The < sign tells the computer to get information from a file.

- The > sign tells the computer to send information to a file.

- The string 2> will redirect all error messages to a file.

```
#!/bin/csh
clear
echo "Employee Data"
echo " "
cat employees.dat
```

Notice how the last line has the `cat` command followed by the filename.

The following example shows you what appears on the screen when this program runs with the `cat` utility.

```
Employee Data

Bob Smith
Mary Jones
```

Of course, this example assumes that someone entered Bob Smith the first time the program was run and Mary Jones the second time!

Chapter 6

Arithmetic, Logical, and Comparison Operators

● ●

In This Chapter

▶ Adding, subtracting, multiplying, and dividing numbers

▶ Using the *not*, *and*, and *or* operators

▶ Comparing values with comparison operators

▶ Establishing precedence for operators

● ●

*A*fter your computer receives information from someone who uses your program, the next step is to do something with the information. For example, you can have your computer calculate a result.

Anytime that you want your computer to modify data, you must tell the computer to perform an *operation* — by using one or more *operators* in your program. UNIX has three categories of operators (each with its own operators):

✔ Arithmetic

✔ Logical

✔ Comparison

Arithmetic Operators

Arithmetic operators transform your expensive computer into one of those pocket calculators that are given away when you sign up for a high interest rate credit card.

These arithmetic operators let your computer add, subtract, multiply, and divide numbers or variables that contain numbers (see Chapter 4 for the scoop on variables). Table 6-1 shows these operators (as if you couldn't figure them out on your own).

Table 6-1	Arithmetic Operators
Operator	*What It Does*
+	Adds two numbers
–	Subtracts two numbers
*	Multiplies two numbers
/	Divides two numbers
%	Divides two numbers and returns only the remainder

Adding two numbers with the + operator

To add two numbers together, use the + operator:

```
@ a = 30
@ b = 10
@ sum = $a + $b
```

Note the spaces around the = signs and around the + operator. Such spacing is true for all constructions of operators.

@ a = 30 tells the computer to create a variable called a and to assign it the value 30.

@ b = 10 tells the computer to create a variable called b and to assign it the value 10.

@ sum = $a + $b tells the computer to create a variable called sum and to assign it the value of a plus the value of b. In this example, the value of sum equals 30 + 10 (which is 40!).

Subtracting two numbers with the – operator

To subtract two numbers, use the - operator:

```
@ Salary = 3000
@ Expenses = 2500
@ MyMoney = $Salary - $Expenses
```

@ Salary = 3000 tells the computer to create a variable called Salary and to assign it the value 3000.

@ Expenses = 2500 tells the computer to create a variable called Expenses and to assign it the value 2500.

@ MyMoney = $Salary - $Expenses tells the computer to create a variable called MyMoney and to assign it the value of Salary minus the value of Expenses. In this example, the value of MyMoney equals 3000 – 2500, or 500.

Multiplying two numbers with the * operator

To multiply two numbers together, use the * operator:

```
@ Salary = 3000
@ Raise = 1.05
@ NewSalary = $Salary * $Raise
```

@ Salary = 3000 tells the computer to create a variable called Salary and to assign it the value 3000.

@ Raise = 1.05 tells the computer to create a variable called Raise and to assign it the value 1.05. (This will give you a 5 percent raise in pay!)

@ NewSalary = $Salary * $Raise tells the computer to create a variable called NewSalary and to assign it the value of Salary times the value of Raise. In this example, the value of NewSalary equals 3000 * 1.05, or 3150.

Dividing two numbers with the / operator

To divide two numbers use the / (forward slash) operator:

```
@ TotalSalary = 100000
@ NumEmployees = 5
@ AvgSalary = $TotalSalary / $NumEmployees
```

Negating numbers with the – operator

The – operator can transform a positive number into a negative number. This process is called *negating a number* and is accomplished by placing the – operator in front of any number or variable that contains a number.

@ AfterTaxes = - 3000

@ AfterTaxes = - 3000 tells the computer to create a variable called AfterTaxes and to assign it the negative value of 3000. In this example, the value of Salary is – 3000.

@ `TotalSalary = 100000` tells the computer to create a variable called `TotalSalary` and to assign it the value 100000.

@ `NumEmployees = 5` tells the computer to create a variable called `NumEmployees` and to assign it the value 5.

@ `AvgSalary = $TotalSalary / $NumEmployees` tells the computer to create a variable called `AvgSalary` and to assign it the value of `TotalSalary` divided by the value of `NumEmployees`. In this example, the value of `AvgSalary` equals 1000000 / 5, or 20000.

Dividing with the % (modulo) operator

To divide two numbers and calculate the remainder, use the % operator. (You probably get the idea by now, right?)

```
@ a = 10
@ b = 3
@ c = 10 % 3
```

@ `a = 10` tells the computer to create a variable called `a` and to assign it the value 10.

@ `b = 3` tells the computer to create a variable called `b` and to assign it the value 3.

@ `c = 10 % 3` tells the computer to create a variable called `c` and to assign it the value equal to the remainder of the value of `b` divided by the value of `a`. In this example, the value of `c` equals 10 % 3, or 1.

Logical Operators

Logical operators are used to tell the computer to evaluate *true* and *false* values. A true value is any value that is not a zero, and a false value is a zero. Table 6-2 shows the common logical operators.

Table 6-2	Logical Operators
Operator	**What It Does**
!	Reverses the logic, like saying "I hope it's going to rain — not."
&&	Variable1 *and* Variable2, like saying "Bob *and* Mary are an item."
||	Variable1 *or* Variable2, like saying "Is Mary *or* Sue dating Bob?"

The ! (not) operator

Thanks to television, there is a new way of saying things today. "I'm going to give you a 20 percent increase in pay — not!" Such a statement gets your hopes up and then slams reality in your face. The first part of the phrase leads you to believe the statement is true. However, this true meaning is reversed to a false meaning by the simple word *not.*

You can change a true statement to false just like I did here by using the ! operator (*not*).

You can also use the ! operator to change a false statement to true. Here's an example:

```
$Salary == 3000
```

With $Salary == 3000, the computer is asked to compare the value of the $Salary variable with the value 3000. (The == is a comparison operator that I explain very soon.) If the variable has the same value, the statement is true. And in this example, just assume that it's true.

```
!$Salary == 3000
```

With !$Salary == 3000, the computer is asked perform the same analysis, which results in a true statement. Then the computer is told to reverse the value of the statement. So instead of the computer saying that the statement is true (which it is), the computer will say the statement is false because of the ! operator.

The && (and) operator

The && operator (*and*) tells the computer to compare two variables. Each variable has either a true or a false value. Based on these values, the computer tells you that the statement is true or false. Here's how it works:

```
BuyCar = LowestPrice && LikeCar
```

The computer decides whether the value of the BuyCar variable is true or false by checking the values of the LowestPrice and LikeCar variables. The && operator tells the computer to return a true value only if the LowestPrice and LikeCar both have a true value.

```
BuyCar      LowestPrice     LikeCar
True        True            True
False       False           False
False       True            False
False       False           True
```

The || (or) operator

The || operator (*or*) tells the computer to compare two variables, each one having a true or false value. Based on these values, the computer will return a true or false value. For example:

```
BuyCar = LowestPrice || LikeCar
```

The computer decides whether the value of the BuyCar variable is true or false by checking the values of the LowestPrice and LikeCar variables. The || operator tells the computer to return a true value only if one or both LowestPrice and LikeCar have a true value.

```
BuyCar      LowestPrice     LikeCar
True        True            True
False       False           False
True        True            False
True        False           True
```

Comparison Operators

Comparison operators tell the computer to compare the values of two numbers or two strings to decide whether they are equal to, not equal to, greater than, or less than one another. Table 6-3 shows the common comparison operators.

Table 6-3	Comparison Operators
Operator	*What It Does*
==	Equal to
!=	Not equal to
>	Greater than
>=	Greater than or equal to
<	Less than
<=	Less than or equal to

ANSI character codes

You understand more than your computer understands. It is hard to believe, but computers only know two numbers—ones and zeros. These are called *binary numbers.*

Binary numbers are ideal for doing math. The computer can do this just like you do with your calculator. However, when it comes to letters and punctuation marks, your computer falls flat on its face. Thanks to the American National Standards Institute (ANSI), your computer can compare our words. They came up with the ANSI character codes that assign each character a set of eight binary numbers. So, when you type the letter A, the computer translates that A to the number 65 (the binary number version, that is).

Now, how does your program know if two words are the same? It subtracts the numeric representation of each letter of both words. If the result is zero, there is a match. For example, if the first letter of both words is A, the program subtracts the numeric equivalent of the letter A (65) in the second word from the numeric equivalent of the letter A (65) in the first word. The result is zero. They match.

The == (equal to) operator

To determine whether two values are the same, use the == operator. (Note that no space is between the two = signs).

```
@ Salary = 3000
@ NewSalary = 2000
@ IsItTheSameMoney = ($Salary == $NewSalary)
```

@ Salary = 3000 tells the computer to create a variable called Salary and to assign it the value 3000.

@ NewSalary = 2000 tells the computer to create a variable called NewSalary and to assign it the value 2000.

@ IsItTheSameMoney = ($Salary == $NewSalary) tells the computer to determine if the value of the Salary variable is equal to the value of the NewSalary variable. If it is, the computer assigns a true value to the variable IsItTheSameMoney; otherwise the computer assigns a false value. Don't worry about the parentheses for now; I just use them here in order to establish a precedence — which is a topic I explain later in this chapter.

The != (not equal to) operator

To determine whether two values are not the same, use the != operator.

```
@ Salary = 3000
@ NewSalary = 2000
@ IsItTheSameMoney = $Salary != $NewSalary
```

@ Salary = 3000 tells the computer to create a variable called Salary and to assign it the value 3000.

@ NewSalary = 2000 tells the computer to create a variable called NewSalary and to assign it the value 2000.

@ IsItTheSameMoney = $Salary != $NewSalary tells the computer to determine if the value of the Salary variable is not equal to the value of the NewSalary variable. If it is not, the computer assigns a true value to the variable IsItTheSameMoney; otherwise the computer assigns a false value.

The > (greater than) operator

To determine if the value of the first variable is greater than the value of the second variable, use the > operator.

```
@ Salary = 3000
@ NewSalary = 2000
@ IsItTheSameMoney = $Salary > $NewSalary
```

@ Salary = 3000 tells the computer to create a variable called Salary and to assign it the value 3000.

@ NewSalary = 2000 tells the computer to create a variable called NewSalary and to assign it the value 2000.

@ IsItTheSameMoney = $Salary > $NewSalary tells the computer to determine if the value of the Salary variable is greater than the value of the NewSalary variable. If it is, the computer assigns a true value to the variable IsItTheSameMoney; otherwise the computer assigns a false value.

The >= (greater than or equal to) operator

To determine if the value of the first variable is greater than or equal to the value of the second variable, use the >= operator.

```
@ Salary = 3000
@ NewSalary = 2000
@ IsItTheSameMoney = $Salary >= $NewSalary
```

@ Salary = 3000 tells the computer to create a variable called Salary and to assign it the value 3000.

@ NewSalary = 2000 tells the computer to create a variable called NewSalary and to assign it the value 2000.

@ IsItTheSameMoney = $Salary >= $NewSalary tells the computer to determine if the value of the Salary variable is greater than or equal to the value of the NewSalary variable. If it is, the computer assigns a true value to the variable IsItTheSameMoney; otherwise the computer assigns a false value.

The < (less than) operator

To determine if the value of the first variable is less than the value of the second variable, use the < operator.

```
@ Salary = 3000
@ NewSalary = 2000
@ IsItTheSameMoney = $Salary < $NewSalary
```

@ Salary = 3000 tells the computer to create a variable called Salary and to assign it the value 3000.

@ NewSalary = 2000 tells the computer to create a variable called NewSalary and to assign it the value 2000.

@ IsItTheSameMoney = $Salary < $NewSalary tells the computer to determine if the value of the Salary variable is less than the value of the NewSalary variable. If it is, the computer assigns a true value to the variable IsItTheSameMoney; otherwise the computer assigns a false value.

The <= (less than or equal to) operator

To determine if the value of the first variable is less than or equal to the value of the second variable, use the <= operator.

```
@ Salary = 3000
@ NewSalary = 2000
@ IsItTheSameMoney = $Salary <= $NewSalary
```

@ Salary = 3000 tells the computer to create a variable called Salary and to assign it the value 3000.

@ NewSalary = 2000 tells the computer to create a variable called NewSalary and to assign it the value 2000.

@ IsItTheSameMoney = $Salary <= $NewSalary tells the computer to determine if the value of the Salary variable is less than or equal to the value of the NewSalary variable. If it is, the computer assigns a true value to the variable IsItTheSameMoney, otherwise the computer assigns a false value.

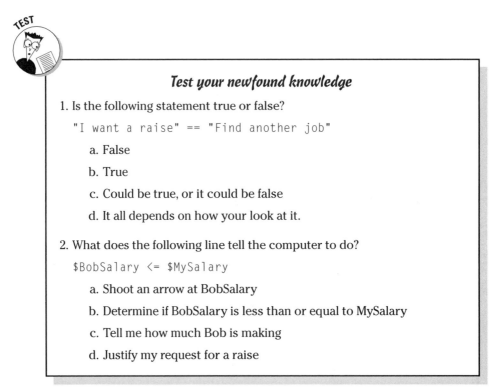

Test your newfound knowledge

1. Is the following statement true or false?

   `"I want a raise" == "Find another job"`

   a. False

   b. True

   c. Could be true, or it could be false

   d. It all depends on how your look at it.

2. What does the following line tell the computer to do?

   `$BobSalary <= $MySalary`

   a. Shoot an arrow at BobSalary

   b. Determine if BobSalary is less than or equal to MySalary

   c. Tell me how much Bob is making

   d. Justify my request for a raise

Give Precedence to Your Operators

Your program won't become confused when you use one operator per instruction. You can say, "Add this value to that value." On the next line of your program you can say, "Subtract this number from that number." Both you and your program understand what you want done.

However, confusion comes when you lump operators together in the same instruction. What answer will your computer give you when it reads the following instruction:

```
@ Total = 6 / 3 + 7 * 5
```

✔ It could be 37:

  2 = 6/3

  35 = 7 * 5

  37 = 2 + 35

✔ It could be 3:

10 = 3 + 7

0.6 = 6 / 10

3 = 0.6 * 5

✔ It could be: 0.1579:

35 = 7 * 5

38 = 3 + 38

0.1579 = 6 / 38

You didn't think simple arithmetic was that complicated. Well, another bunch of whiz kids, who were around long before the guys at Bell Labs, came up with an easy solution. They decided to list which operation is to be performed before other operations. This list is called the *precedence table,* shown in Table 6-4 (but don't worry about the operators I haven't explained — I just wanted to give you the complete table).

By the way. The answer to 6 / 3 + 7 * 5 is 37. See if you can figure out why by using the precedence table.

Table 6-4	Precedence Table
Operator	*Order Of Precedence*
( )	1
~	2
!	3
*	4
/	4
%	4
+	5
–	5
<<	6
>>	6
<=	7
>=	7
=~	7

(continued)

Table 6-4 *(continued)*

Operator	Order Of Precedence
!=	7
==	8
!=	8
=~	8
!~	8
&	9
^	10
		11
&&	12
			13

Programmers don't memorize the precedence table. Instead, they explicitly tell the computer which operation to perform first by surrounding that portion of the instruction with parentheses. Although most programmers use parentheses for clarity, you may come across code written by a programmer who didn't use parentheses. Therefore, you may need to reference the precedence table sometimes.

Here's how to use parentheses in case you want the result to be 3 instead of 37:

```
@ Total = (6 / (3 + 7)) * 5
```

The computer performs the addition operation first because this is surrounded by a set of parentheses.

But there are two sets of parentheses! Correct, so the computer looks in the innermost set of parentheses first, which is the addition: 10 = 3 + 7

After the addition is performed, the division is done next. This is because the division is outside of the inner parentheses but still within the outer set of parentheses: 0.6 = 6 / 10

And finally the multiplication is performed: 3 = 0.6 * 5

Chapter 7

Using Comments

●●

●●

*Y*our UNIX program may be clear to you, but let your friends take a look at it, and they may spend several hours trying to figure out what's happening.

After a program is written, some programmers put it aside, work on a different project, and then come back to the program. Chances are that if you do this you will have to study your own code to be able to recall what you wanted your program to tell the computer to do.

How can you keep from forgetting what your UNIX program is supposed to do? There is only one solution: Place comments throughout your program. A *comment* is a line in your program that tells you what's happening in your code. Your computer ignores any comments it encounters, as though it's saying, "Keep your remarks to yourself — you already gave me instructions."

How to Create Comments

You create a comment in a program by typing # (the number sign) anywhere on the line. Characters between the number sign and the end of the line are ignored by your program. Here are examples of comments:

```
#This is the beginning of my program
clear #This clears the screen
```

The first line in this example doesn't tell the computer anything to do. This comment line does tell, however, to those reading the program that this is the beginning of the program. The second line instructs the computer to clear the screen and has a comment for anyone who reads the program (just in case they need help!).

You can use as many comment lines as you want. Just make sure that each line begins with a # sign.

Make Your Comments Worthwhile

The main reason for placing comments in a program is to make it easy for you to remember what you want the computer to do with your instructions. Most programmers use comments at the beginning of important sections of their programs.

To introduce the purpose of your program to who may read it, you should always place comments at the beginning of your programs. (You never know when you might want to share your programming secrets with a friend.) Although you can create any kind of introductory comments you want for your program, you should include at least the information in this list:

✔ Program name

✔ Programmer's name

✔ Purpose of the program

✔ Name of the intended user of the program

✔ Date on which the program was written (and sometimes the time)

✔ Date of the last change that was made to the program

✔ Name of the programmer who made the last change

Now that you know what you should include at the top of your program, see how your program should look with this information in place. The following example of commented code incorporates all the information in the preceding list:

```
#Title: Regional Reporting Program
#Programmer: Mary Jones
#Purpose: Provide business tracking for each regional office.
#Primary user: All regional office managers and their staff.
#Originally written: 12/26/95
#Last changed: 2/4/96
#Changed by: Roger Smith
```

Use comments throughout your program to identify key actions the computer will take. In the following example, the computer is instructed to call a subprogram named menu1, and the comment reminds you of this action:

```
#Display the opening screen
menu1
```

The name of the subprogram `menu1` doesn't provide much information. You can guess that it has something to do with a menu, but which one? And anyone reading your code will have even less of an idea. That question is answered by the comment in front of the instruction.

When you're trying to decide whether to use a comment in your program, follow this rule of thumb: When in doubt, add the comment.

Make Your Comments Easy to Read

Keep in mind that you and your friends will probably be reading your UNIX programs (so you had better watch what you say). You can make your program much easier to read if you use blank lines to separate chunks of your program.

In addition to making your comments understandable to anyone who reads them, you must also present them in a clear way. Look at the following example to see how difficult it is to identify the different sections in the program:

```
#Title: Regional Reporting Program
#Programmer: Mary Jones
#Purpose: Provide business tracking for each regional office.
#Primary User: All regional office managers and their staff.
#Originally Written: 12/26/95
#Last Changed: 2/4/96
#Changed By: Roger Smith
#Change these values for each region
setenv REGIONAL_OFFICE Boston
setenv REGIONAL_MGR 'Mary Smith'
setenv REGIONAL_SALES 1000000
#Display the opening screen
menu1
```

Can you quickly see where comments end and the code begins? Probably not. Now compare the preceding example with the following one:

```
#Title: Regional Reporting Program
#Programmer: Mary Jones
#Purpose: Provide business tracking for each regional office.
#Primary User: All regional office managers and their staff.
#Originally Written: 12/26/98
#Last Changed: 2/4/99
#Changed By: Roger Smith

#Change these values for each region
setenv REGIONAL_OFFICE Boston
setenv REGIONAL_MGR 'Mary Smith'
setenv REGIONAL_SALES 1000000

#Display the opening screen
menu1
```

This example is much easier to read because blank lines are used to break up the code into sections. You add blank lines to your program by inserting a carriage return (also called a *hard return*) on a line that doesn't contain any text. The easiest way to insert a hard return is to move the cursor to the end of a line of text and press the Enter key. Rather than type text on the line, press the Enter key again. Voilà — a blank line!

How to Disable a Pesky Instruction

Beware! Bugs can work their way into your program. A *bug* is an error in your program, and sometimes it is hard to uncover. Suppose that you have written a program to tell your computer to do something, but the computer doesn't do it. You have a bug in your program! What do you do? Here are your choices:

- ✔ Scream, "I hate computers!" This technique doesn't do anything to get your program to work, of course, but it certainly can relieve some of your frustrations.

- ✔ Test your program to determine which instruction isn't working. Keep in mind that the computer does what you tell it to do. Probably, you have simply given it an incorrect instruction.

Comments can be used to disable instructions in your program. Although programmers use a number of techniques to locate bugs in their programs (I discuss these techniques in-depth in Chapter 18), most methods consist of these basic steps:

1. Disable an instruction.

2. Test the program.

3. Review the results.

You can disable a part of your program by placing the number sign (#) at the beginning of the line that contains the instruction.

Suppose that you run a program (a snippet of which is in the following example) and for some reason it displays an incorrect regional sales value. As you inspect your code, you see — and suspect — an instruction that creates a REGIONAL_SALES environment variable that has a value of 1000000. Could this be the problem? You could erase this instruction and rerun the program to see what happens. If this particular instruction isn't causing the problem, however, you must remember which instruction you deleted so that you can add it to your program again.

```
#Change these values for each region
setenv REGIONAL_OFFICE Boston
setenv REGIONAL_MGR 'Mary Smith'
setenv REGIONAL_SALES 1000000

#Display the opening screen
menu1
```

A better method is to place a comment sign (#) as the first character of the instruction.

```
#Change these values for each region
setenv REGIONAL_OFFICE Boston
setenv REGIONAL_MGR 'Mary Smith'
#setenv REGIONAL_SALES 1000000

#Display the opening screen
menu1
```

The computer then ignores the instruction setenv REGIONAL_SALES 1000000 just as though you had erased it. To restore the instruction, all you have to do is remove the comment sign.

Test your newfound knowledge

1. What is the number sign (#) used for in your program?

    a. To have the program call your mom

    b. To tell the computer to ignore all the characters that follow the number sign on the line

    c. To create a tic-tac-toe board on the screen

    d. To make your program look attractive to your boss

2. Why should you use comments in your program?

    a. To tell a private joke to your friend who's reading your program

    b. To summarize how your program works

    c. To insert a secret code so that you can identify your program if someone steals it

    d. To have the computer call the FBI someone illegally uses your program

Part III
Making Decisions

The 5th Wave

Re·al Pro·gram·mers

By Rich Tennant

ELEVATOR CAPACITY
2100 LBS.

Real Programmers love to talk "computer-eze" while ordinary citizens are listening.

In this part . . .

Your program contains many instructions for the computer. Simply stated, programs contain a list of instructions that the computer follows one after the other.

But what if some of those instructions should be followed only when a particular condition exists? For this situation, you must tell the computer to make a decision.

Your computer's decision-making capability lets you build complex programs that allow your computer to perform mundane tasks that you'd get stuck doing.

In this part, you examine how you instruct your computer to make decisions.

Chapter 8

The `if`, `if else`, and `if else if` Statements

- -

In This Chapter

▶ Specifying a condition

▶ Using the `if` statement

▶ Using the `if else` statement

▶ Using the `if else if` statement

- -

*D*ecisions, decisions, decisions. We're always asked to make decisions.

— Where do you want to go on vacation? To my mother's or to Hawaii?

Some decisions are obvious choices, but even those no-brainers are based upon prevailing conditions.

— Do we have enough money for a trip to the island?

And if conditions are not right, even the most desirable choice is just a memory.

— It's Mom's again this year.

UNIX programming also can make decisions by checking conditions and then reaching a conclusion.

Conditions

A condition must be a value that is *true* or *false*. You have enough money for the trip to Hawaii or you don't. There is no room for an "almost enough money." A condition takes the form of

> ✔ A single variable
>
> ✔ An expression

Say that you have all your money in your wallet. We can call the variable *wallet* and the value of the variable is thus the *amount of money* that you have in your wallet. So, do you have enough money for the trip to Hawaii? Look in your wallet. You say that there is not much money in it? You're broke! Therefore, the value of the wallet variable is zero — which means you don't have enough money for the trip. The condition is false.

However, let's say that you have a good deal of money in the wallet. Is it enough money for the trip? You'd ask yourself if the amount of money in the wallet is equal to or greater than $10,000 (the amount you need for the trip). This is an expression that results in either a true or false answer.

The condition as a single variable

The value of a single variable must be either *true* or *false*. A true value is represented as a nonzero value, and a false value is a zero value. Here are a couple of ways to determine if the value of a variable is either true or false. The first method is to explicitly check the value of the variable. For example

```
if ($HaveEnoughMoney == 1)
```

Your program checks if the value of the variable is true or false by using the equal sign (==).

If you can have your program check if a condition is true, you can also have your program check if the value of the variable is false. Here's how it's done:

```
if ($HaveEnoughMoney != 0)
```

The != (not equal) operator tells your program to reverse the logic. When the == operator is used, your program checks if the variable is true. Place the != operator in the expression, and your program checks if the variable is not true, which is false.

The condition as an expression

A condition can be an *expression*. An expression tells your program to perform an operation on information. For example, you can ask the program to check if the value of a variable, such as your bank balance, is more than a specific amount. In this case, the result of an expression is either true or false, as shown here:

```
if ($BankBalance > 3000)
```

Other operators useful for testing a condition

Whenever you need to tell your program to check if a condition is true or false, you need to create an expression that uses an appropriate operator. Here is a list of the operators that you'd use to test conditions in your program. These operators are for integers and for strings.

==	Equals	>=	Greater than or equal to
!=	Does not equal	<	Less than
>	Greater than	<=	Less than or equal to

Your program checks to see if the value of BankBalance is greater than 3000. This expression results in one of two possible values, true or false. A bank balance greater than 3000 means the expression is true (and the trip is on); otherwise the expression is false.

An expression that contains a string can also be either true or false. In the following example, your program determines if the variable GoingToHawaii contains the string Yes. If the string exists, the expression is true; otherwise the expression is false.

```
if ($GoingToHawaii == "Yes")
```

The if *Statement*

You use an if statement whenever you need your program to check whether or not a condition is true or false. An if statement simply tells your program that "If the condition is true, follow these instructions; otherwise, skip these instructions."

A true condition causes your program to follow a set of instructions. A false condition causes your program to ignore that set of instructions.

Cut to the chase and see how this all comes together.

```
if (Condition)then
    Instruction
endif
```

Basically, your program is told to follow the Instruction if a certain Condition exists — meaning the Condition is true.

Regardless of the Condition, the Condition must always be true or false.

Here are some real-life examples. The first one tells your program to check if the box is full. The box can only hold 100 cookies (something dear to my stomach).

```
if ($Quantity == 100)then
   echo "The box is full."
endif
```

This statement tells your program to look at the variable called Quantity and decide if the value is 100 cookies. If that is true, your program takes the message The box is full. and displays the message on the screen:

```
The box is full.
```

However, if the value is not 100 cookies, your program skips this instruction and moves to the instruction that follows the endif. This endif is a reserved word that has a special meaning to your program (because it ends the if statement).

Try another example. In this case, your program must check to see if the box is full and check to see if there are any sufficient boxes available. Both conditions must be true for your program to report back that you can't package any more cookies.

```
if ($Quantity == 100 && $AvailableBoxes < 1)then
   echo "The box is full and there are no more boxes."
endif
```

This statement tells your program to look at the variable called Quantity and decide if the value is 100 cookies. Your program also looks at the variable called AvailableBoxes to see if the value is less than 1. If both conditions are true, your program displays the message The box is full and there are no more boxes. on the screen.

However, if the value is not 100 cookies, and boxes are remaining, your program skips this instruction and moves to the instruction that follows the endif reserved word.

A bunch of instructions can be placed within the if statement; your program obeys these instructions only if the condition is true.

The if else *Statement*

The if statement enables your program to make a decision dependent upon a condition and then to follow a specific set of rules if the condition is true.

A problem with using the if statement is that another set of instructions may be required to be obeyed if the condition is false. You could use another if statement and tell your program to follow the other set of instructions if the condition is false. But there is an easier way! Use something called an if else statement. Here is the easiest if else statement:

```
if (Condition)then
        Instruction1
    else
        Instruction2
endif
```

This statement tells your program to obey the first group of instructions if the Condition is true . . . but to obey the second group of instructions if the Condition is false.

Here's a pop quiz to see if you've been paying attention. How would you modify the following to tell your program to display the message The box is not full.?

```
if ($Quantity == 100) then
    echo "The box is full."
endif
```

You can modify this statement in two ways. Each method depends on how the condition is expressed. If you leave the condition unchanged, you get this:

```
if ($Quantity == 100) then
        echo "The box is full."
    else
        echo "The box is not full."
endif
```

However, you could use the condition $Quantity != 100 to get the following:

```
if ($Quantity != 100) then
        echo "The box is not full."
    else
        echo "The box is full."
endif
```

Feel free to use either type of the if else statements. Both are acceptable, and the one you decide to use is up to your preference.

You can place a whole bunch of instructions between the expression and else reserved word and another whole bunch between the else and endif reserved words. The following example shows how the on-screen messages are expanded when you place more instructions.

```
if ($Quantity != 100)then
    echo "The box is full."
    echo "Sorry, you'll have to stop."
  else
    echo "The box is not full."
     echo "Keep going!"
endif
```

The if else if *Statement*

Be careful! Your program blindly follows your instructions when the condition is false. The second bunch of instructions are obeyed without your program asking a question. Sometimes you don't want this blind obedience to happen. Instead, you want your program to make another decision before following the second bunch of instructions.

You can have your computer make another decision by using the if else if statement. This statement looks confusing at first but is fairly easy to understand after you get used to it. Here's a simple if else if statement:

```
if (Condition1)then
    Instruction1
  else if (Condition2)then
    Instruction2
endif
```

In this statement, your program obeys the first group of instructions if Condition1 is true. However, if Condition1 is false, your program determines if Condition2 is true. If Condition2 is true, your program obeys the second group of instructions. If Condition2 is false, your program skips the second group of instructions.

Whenever you use the if statement, your program obeys at least one group of instructions. However, when you use the if else if statement, there is always a chance that your program will skip both groups of instructions. Here's an example:

```
if ($Quantity == 100) then
     echo "The box is full."
   else if ($Quantity == 95)then
     echo "You can add 5 cookies to the box."
endif
```

So what happens if the value of Quantity is 95 in the preceding example? Your program determines the value of the first condition and sees that the expression $Quantity == 100 is false.

Then your program determines the value of the second condition and sees that the expression $Quantity == 95 is true, so your program displays the message: You can add 5 cookies to the box.

Be careful when you answer this question. What happens if the value of Quantity is 94?

Your program checks the first condition $Quantity == 100 and determines that the expression is false. Your program ignores the first bunch of instructions. Your program then checks the second condition $Quantity == 95. This, too, is false. Your program ignores the second bunch of instructions.

The end of the if else if statement is reached. None of the conditions was true, so your program did not obey any instructions!

Making multiple choices with if else if

You can have your program handle multiple possibilities by having more else if conditions in your program to check the additional conditions. Here is the simplest way to use multiple if else if conditions:

```
if (Condition1)then
     Instruction1
   else if (Condition2)then
     Instruction2
   else if (Condition3)then
     Instruction3
end if
```

In this statement, your program is told to obey the first group of instructions if Condition1 is true. However, if Condition1 is false, your program determines if Condition2 is true. If Condition2 is true, your program obeys the second group of instructions. If Condition2 is false, your program determines if Condition3 is true. If Condition3 is true, your program obeys the third group of instructions — or otherwise skips the third group of instructions.

Watch out! All the conditions can be false, so your program may not obey any of the instructions within the if else if statement.

Caution! The more else if lines that are used in your program, the more confusing it will be to read the entire if else if statement. (It will be worse than reading instructions for filling out your taxes — unless you like jumping around the instruction booklet.)

Making sure that UNIX follows at least one group of instructions

Imagine having a gigantic if else if statement only to find out that no instructions are obeyed. This can happen in real life. You can avoid such a disaster by placing an else statement at the end of the if else if statement. Here's a sample:

```
if (Condition1)then
     Instruction1
   else if (Condition2)then
     Instruction2
   else if (Condition3)then
     Instruction3
   else
     Instruction4
endif
```

In this statement, your program is told to obey the first group of instructions if Condition1 is true. However, if Condition1 is false, your program determines if Condition2 is true. If Condition2 is true, your program obeys the second group of instructions. If Condition2 is false, your program determines if Condition3 is true. If Condition3 is true, your program obeys the third group of instructions — otherwise your program obeys the fourth group of instructions.

Test your newfound knowledge

1. How many instructions can you place within an `if` statement?

   a. 24

   b. As many as you want

   c. 0

   d. As many as you can fit on the screen

2. How can you be sure that your program will follow at least one instruction in an `if else if` statement?

   a. Write only simple instructions for your program.

   b. Keep running the program until it follows an instruction.

   c. Place an `else` statement at the end of the `if else if` statement.

   d. Complain to the system administrator.

Chapter 9

The switch case Statement

*Y*ou could run into a problem when you tell your computer to make a decision that has many possibilities. Say, for example, that you want your computer to do something unique with each of five regional offices in your company. Your program requires a bunch of if else if statements like this:

```
if ($region == "New York")then
    echo "Hello, Bob"
else if ($region == "Chicago")then
    echo "Hello, Mary"
else if ($region == "Los Angeles")then
    echo "Hello, Joan"
else if ($region == "Dallas")then
    echo "Hello, Mike"
else if ($region == "Indianapolis")then
    echo "Hello, Tom"
endif
```

This is a mess to read — although your computer can read it just fine. But as for you, try to imagine tracking 20 if statements if you needed to update 20 regional offices!

The switch case Statement

Say that you want to have your program display a different message on the screen if the program is being used in New York, Chicago, Los Angeles, Dallas, and Indianapolis. When the program begins, you could have it ask the user to enter the name of the city; then you could have your program match the name of the city with those cities for which you created a special message.

As you saw in the preceding chapter, you could use a series of `if else if` statements to direct your program to compare the names of the cities. However, this code becomes difficult to read, especially if you have a long list of cities. A better way to do the same thing is to use the `switch case` statement.

The `switch case` statement tells your program to match values that are associated with a series of cases (`case` is a reserved word) against a single value associated with the `switch` reserved word. The `switch case` statement looks like this:

```
switch (VariableName)
    case value1:
        Instruction
        breaksw

    case value2:
        Instruction
        breaksw
endsw
```

This statement — beginning with the `switch` reserved word and ending with the `endsw` reserved word — tells your program to look at the value of `VariableName`. If this value is equal to `value1`, the program follows the first set of instructions. If this is equal to `value2`, the program follows the second set of instructions. The program follows all the instructions that appear between the `case` reserved word and the `breaksw` reserved word if there is a match.

In case you haven't noticed, a colon (:) follows each `case` statement.

Now I replace the `if` statement used at the beginning of the chapter with the `switch case` statement.

```
switch ($region)
    case "New York":
        echo "Hello, Bob."
        breaksw
    case "Chicago":
        echo "Hello, Mary."
        breaksw
    case "Los Angeles":
        echo "Hello, Joan."
        breaksw
    case "Dallas":
        echo "Hello, Mike."
        breaksw
    case "Indianapolis":
```

```
        echo "Hello, Tom."
        breaksw
endsw
```

This code is much easier to read (for humans) because repetitive words such as `else if` are eliminated. You can stuff as many values in this statement as you need. In effect, the `switch case` statement streamlines your program and makes it easy for you and your fellow humans to read.

You must keep a few things in mind, however, when using the `switch case` statement. (You knew it was too good to be true, right?)

- ✔ The `switch` value must be one or more characters. Numeric values are not allowed.

- ✔ A variable or a string value can be used as a `switch` value.

- ✔ A variable or a string value can be a `case` value.

Making the Program Do Something by `default`

Your program can find itself unable to match the `switch` value when you don't supply it with the necessary matching value (whoops!). Sometimes this situation doesn't matter if you supply the `switch` value. However, a problem could arise if someone else supplies the `switch` value.

For example, say that another regional office opened and you didn't have time to change your program to handle the new region. (Maybe you just misplaced that memo.) Your program will run fine. It simply ignores the new region because it didn't match any `case` value that you gave it.

You can have your computer act as your backstop by using the `default` reserved word. Here's an example of how you can use `default`:

```
switch ($region)
   case "New York":
      echo "Hello, Bob."
      breaksw
   case "Chicago":
      echo "Hello, Mary."
      breaksw
```

(continued)

(continued)

```
    case "Los Angeles":
        echo "Hello, Joan."
        breaksw
    case "Dallas":
        echo "Hello, Mike."
        breaksw
    case "Indianapolis":
        echo "Hello, Tom."
        breaksw
    default:
        echo "Sorry, your region is not on my list."
endsw
```

This code tells your program to display the appropriate greeting if the value of $region is equal to New York, Chicago, Los Angeles, Dallas, or Indianapolis. However, if your program can't match the value of $region, it displays the last set of instructions: Sorry, your region is not on my list.

The switch case *Statement in the User Interface*

The most common use for the switch case statement is with your program's user interface. When your program displays your menu, it has to wait for someone to enter a key from the keyboard. The person using your program makes a selection, and then your program reads the selection and compares it to specific values using the switch case statement.

Say that you want to create an electronic telephone book. I'll keep it simple and say that you want two functions: display a telephone number and add a telephone number. First, these functions are displayed on the screen; then the program reads the user's selection from the keyboard. You use the switch case statement to compare the user's selection with available functions. In this example, the program simply displays a message telling which selection the user made. These messages would be replaced by other instructions in a more complex version of this program, of course.

```
#!/bin/csh
clear
echo " "
echo "        The Telephone Book "
echo " "
```

```
echo "        1. Display A Telephone Number "
echo "        2. Add A New Telephone Number "
echo " "
echo "        Q Quit "
echo " "
echo "     Enter your selection: "
echo " "
set selection = $<
switch ($selection)
   case "1":
      echo "You want to display a telephone number."
      breaksw
   case "2":
      echo "You want to add a new telephone number."
      breaksw
   case "q":
      exit 0
      breaksw
   case "Q":
      exit 0
      breaksw
   default:
      echo "You made an invalid selection."
endsw
```

Don't worry about the big space that you see between some quoatation marks and the beginning of the on-screen display with the echo command (such as the fourth line of this preceding code) — that space (and the quotes) don't print anyway. I just indented the text to make it easier to read.

To avoid any problem with the user trying to exit your program, you may want to indicate that either lowercase or uppercase letters are fine. In this preceding example, notice that I gave q or Q as a proper way to quit the program.

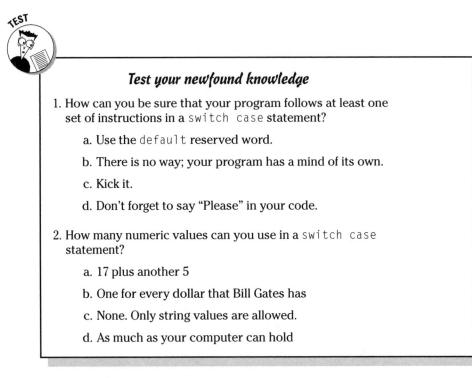

Test your newfound knowledge

1. How can you be sure that your program follows at least one set of instructions in a `switch case` statement?

    a. Use the `default` reserved word.

    b. There is no way; your program has a mind of its own.

    c. Kick it.

    d. Don't forget to say "Please" in your code.

2. How many numeric values can you use in a `switch case` statement?

    a. 17 plus another 5

    b. One for every dollar that Bill Gates has

    c. None. Only string values are allowed.

    d. As much as your computer can hold

Chapter 10

Nested Control Structures

● ●

In This Chapter

▶ Using nested control structures with `if`

▶ Using nested control structures with `switch case`

▶ Indenting nested statements

● ●

*D*id you ever receive a gift in a big box? Quickly you opened it only to find a slightly smaller box inside. Then you opened it, and another, smaller box was inside. This continued until you finally found your present (and I hope it wasn't a hunk of coal).

For programming, the concept of placing one box inside another is called *nesting*. Nesting also occurs when you combine more than one `if` statement together or when you combine more than one `switch case` statement together.

Nesting with `if`

Normally, an `if` statement has one or more sets of instructions, such as this sample that displays a personal greeting to the regional manager of the New York office.

```
if ($region == "New York") then
    echo "Hello, Bob."
else
    echo "Sorry, your region is not on my list."
endif
```

Another way to write the preceding program is to replace the `if` statement with the `switch` statement, as shown here:

```
switch ($region)
   case "New York":
      echo "Hello, Bob."
      breaksw
   default:
      echo "Sorry, your region is not on my list."
endsw
```

Instead of placing a bunch of instructions in the if statement or the switch case statement, you can stuff an if statement and a switch case statement within other if statements and switch case statements. Here's how it's done with the if statement:

```
if ($region == "New York")
   if ($RegionalMgr == "Bob")
      echo "Hello, Bob."
endif
```

The program looks at the value of $region. If the value of $region is New York, the program then looks at the value of $RegionalMgr. If the value of $RegionalMrg is Bob, the program then displays a message greeting Bob.

Nesting with switch case

The same nesting method can be used with the switch case statement. Take a look at this in action:

```
switch ($region)
   case "New York":
      switch ($RegionalMgr)
         case "Bob":
            echo "Hello, Bob."
         breaksw
      endsw
endsw
```

The program looks at the value of $region. If the value of $region is New York, the program then looks at the value of $RegionalMgr. If the value of $RegionalMrg is Bob, the program then follows the instruction and greets Bob.

Don't forget that the case statement is followed by a colon (:).

Making Nesting Statements Easy (for You) to Read

Your computer doesn't care how many if statements or switch case statements that you place inside one another. However, *you* will care whenever you read your program. You can easily become lost reading a program that has multiple nesting statements.

My advice is to indent each nested statement. Indentation isn't a requirement of UNIX, but it is a good style to use when you write a UNIX program. It makes reading your program a lot easier than if you jumble all the nested statement together.

Here's what the code looks like without indenting:

```
switch ($region)
case "New York":
switch ($RegionalMgr)
case "Bob":
echo "Hello, Bob."
breaksw
endsw
endsw
```

Your computer won't have any difficulty reading this program. However, you'll spend a few puzzling minutes matching the nested statements.

By the way, you don't even need a test for this chapter.

Part IV
Loops and Loops

The 5th Wave   By Rich Tennant

Re·al Pro·gram·mers

INVALID CODE. YOU ✻#✱! WALNUT BRAIN!

Real Programmers strive to insult users with error messages.

In this part . . .

Your program contains instructions that tell the computer what to do. Many times those instructions are given just once, such as when you need to display a welcome message for the user.

But sometimes you must tell your computer the same instruction or instructions over and over again. You *could* copy those lines of instructions to new lines in your program.

However, a better way is to simply tell your computer to repeat instructions that are already in your program. This procedure is called *looping*. In this part, you find out how to make loops in your program.

Chapter 11

The while Loop

The while loop works like a group of people caught in the rain, standing under the awning of a store. Every so often, they check to see if it's still raining. While it is still raining, the people stay put. Otherwise, they begin walking toward the car.

You may have your program continue to wait for the user to enter the correct response to a question before continuing with the program. Each time a response is given, the program checks it against the correct response. If there isn't a match, the user is told that he gave the wrong answer, and the program returns to the top of the loop to wait for the next response from the user.

A while loop looks like this:

```
while (Condition)
    Instruction
end
```

The Condition must be a variable or expression that results in a true or false value. And many instructions can be placed in a while loop.

Deciding When to Use a while Loop

When you write a program, you list all the instructions that you want the computer to follow in the order in which you want the instructions to be followed. However, there are times when you want some of those instructions repeated. Instead of writing such instructions over again, you can place them within a loop.

Use a while loop when you need to repeat a group of instructions — as long as a condition is true. For example, if you need to prompt the user to enter a correct password, your group of instructions continues to execute until the user enters the correct password.

Don't use a while loop if you don't want the group of instructions repeated continuously. Say that you want to display the same message on the screen whenever someone makes an error using your program. Although the instructions needed to display the message are repeated in the program, they are repeated only when an error occurs. Placing these instructions in a while loop causes the program to continually display the message. The best way to handle this problem is to place these instructions in a subprogram (see Chapter 14) and then call the subprogram whenever you need to display the message.

Using a while *Loop in Your UNIX Code*

When your program sees a while loop, it checks the condition. It answers the question, "Is this condition true or is it false?". Only if the condition is true does your program read the instructions that you put in the while loop.

The following code shows a while loop in action:

```
set raining = "1"
while ($raining == "1")
    echo "Still raining."
end
```

This is what is happening:

set raining = "1" tells your program to create a string variable called $raining and assign it the value 1. This indicates a true value.

while ($raining == "1") tells your program to check if the value of $raining is still 1. If true, this means that it is still raining.

echo "Still raining." tells your program to display the message on the screen only if it is still raining.

end tells your program that this is the end of the while loop.

Of course, you would need more instructions in this example to make it a working program. For example, in the preceding block of code, your program keeps displaying the message Still raining. because the value of $raining never changes. This is called an *endless loop*. The condition in the while statement is always true.

You need to add instructions that check to see if it is raining. These instructions are placed within the while loop and change the value of $raining to 0 if it stops raining.

Using a while *loop to create a menu*

It's common to use a while loop to create a menu interface. In any program menu, the program user expects to be able to

1. See a menu

2. Make a selection

3. Have the program do something

4. Return to the menu to make further selections

The easiest way to do this menu stuff is to have all these instructions inside a while loop. Each time the program finishes doing what the user requests, the program returns to the while loop and starts all over again. Take a look at this:

```
#!/bin/csh
set flag = "1"
while ($flag == "1")
    clear
    echo " "
    echo "The Telephone Book "
    echo " "
    echo "1. Display A Telephone Number "
    echo "2. Add A New Telephone Number "
    echo " "
    echo "Q Quit "
    echo " "
    echo "Enter your selection: "
    echo " "
    set selection = $<
    switch ($selection)
        case "1":
            #Run the subprogram to display a phone number
            getnum
            breaksw
        case "2":
            #Run the subprogram to add a new phone number
            addnum
            breaksw
```

(continued)

(continued)

```
    case "q":
        $flag = "0"
        breaksw
    case "Q":
        $flag = "0"
        breaksw
    default:
        echo "You made an invalid selection. Try again."
    endsw
end
```

`#!/bin/csh` tells the computer that this is a C shell script. `set flag = "1"` creates a string variable called `$flag` and assigns it the value 1.

Next, the program evaluates the expression in the `while` statement to see if the value of `$flag` is 1.

If so, the program displays the menu and waits for a user to enter a character at the keyboard; this character is stuffed into the `$selection` variable. The program compares the value stored in `$selection` with all possible values using the `switch case` statement.

If a match is found, the program runs a subprogram — but only if the subprogram exists. In this example, an error would occur because you didn't write those subprograms. For example, `getnum` is the name of a subprogram that is run when the user selects the first option on the menu. The subprogram returns to this part of the program after the subprogram finishes and continues with instructions in the `while` loop.

Notice that the program looks for both upper and lowercase 'Q'. This is because the user could enter 'Q' — to quit the program — in either upper or lowercase.

However, if the program doesn't find a match, it tells the user to try another selection. The program repeats this process until the user selects the quit option. When this occurs, the value of `$flag` is changed to 0 and the computer exits the loop the next time it checks the value of `$flag`.

Using a `while` *loop to create a timing loop*

You'll probably come across a problem when you want the program to pause before executing the next group of instructions. For example, you may have a program that displays a series of messages on the screen automatically. Each message appears on the screen for a specific amount of time before the program changes to the next message — a kind of slide show without all the fancy type that you find in a Windows program.

The trick is to make the program pause long enough for someone to read the message. The way you can do this is to use a timing loop. *A timing loop* is a simple while loop where the only instruction within the loop is an instruction to add 1 to a variable. Take a look at this timing loop:

```
set counter = 0
   while ($counter < 1000)
     $counter = $counter + 1
   end
```

In this example, the program stores 0 in a variable called counter, and then the program enters the while loop. The single instruction within the while loop adds 1 to the value of the counter and stores the new value back in the counter variable. The while loop continues to count until the value of the counter variable is 999 — at which time the program leaves the loop.

You can adjust the length of the pause by increasing or decreasing the value in the while condition. In this example, the value of in the while condition is 1000. Increase this value to increase the pause and decrease this value to decrease the pause.

Using a while loop to create a flashing message

Whenever you really want to catch the eye of the user and make sure that your message is read, have your message flash on the screen by using a while loop. First, you instruct the program to display the message on the screen. Next, you start a timing loop (see the preceding section). This process causes your program to pause for a specific length of time. Finally you clear the message from the screen and return to the beginning of the loop. Let's see it in action:

```
set counter1 = 0
while ($counter1 < 6 )
   echo "Warning: There's a bug in your program."
   set counter2 = 0
   while ($counter2 < 1000)
     $counter2 = $counter2 + 1
   end
   clear
   $counter1 = $counter1 + 1
end
```

Notice that I use two `while` loops in this program. The first `while` loop causes the message to flash five times. Each time the message is flashed on the screen, the program adds 1 to the variable `counter1`. When `counter1` has a value of 6, the program exits the first `while` loop.

Each time the message is displayed, the program pauses by entering the second `while` loop. Simply, the program counts to 1000. You can change this value to any number. The higher the number, the slower the message will flash. And the lower the number, the faster the message will flash.

Avoiding Endless `while` Loops

If the condition of the `while` loop is false, your program doesn't execute any of the instructions inside the `while` loop. This means that the instructions inside the `while` loop are never repeated. In fact, they are never even executed. (And after all that work writing this code!) Here's an example:

```
set raining = "0"
while ($raining == "1")
    echo "Still raining."
end
```

Your program will not display the message because the value of $raining is not 1. Instructions inside the `while` loop are skipped, and the program continues on the line that follows the `end` reserved word, which in this case is the end of the program.

If the condition of the `while` loop is true, the program executes all the instructions in the `while` loop at least once.

If the condition of the `while` loop is always true, the program again executes all the instructions in the `while` loop. Your program doesn't stop this until you or the administrator who is responsible for your computer stops the program. Again, this is the infamous endless loop.

No cool programmer wants to have an endless loop in a program. You can avoid this situation by making sure that at least one instruction in the `while` loop changes the true or false value of the condition used in the `while` loop. Here's how it's done:

```
#!/bin/csh
set raining = "1"
while ($raining == "1")
    clear
    echo " "
```

```
    echo "Is it raining? "
    echo " "
    echo "1. Yes "
    echo "2. No "
    echo " "
    echo "Enter your selection: "
    echo " " set raining = $<
end
echo "It stopped raining."
```

#!/bin/csh tells the program that this is a C shell script.

set raining = "1" tells the computer to create a string variable called $raining and assign it the value 1.

while ($raining == "1") tells the program to check if the value of $raining is 1. If so, the program executes the following instructions.

clear tells the program to clear the screen.

The echo stuff displays a menu.

raining $< waits for the user to make a selection, and then assigns the selection to the $raining variable.

The program returns to the top of the while loop and checks to see if the value of $raining is 1. If the value hasn't changed, the instructions are executed again.

If the value is not 1, the instructions are not executed again. The program jumps to the last instruction in the program and displays It stopped raining. on the screen.

Of course, the user could enter a character other than a 1 or 2. If this happened, the program would treat that value as if the user had selected 2. The value of $raining no longer is 1, therefore the program follows the same instructions as if it is not raining.

Don't bunch up instructions you place in a while loop. If you do, you'll spend hours trying to understand what you told the program to do (although your program has no trouble reading your code whether you indent it or not). Always indent lines of instructions so that each instruction is grouped with other instructions used to perform the same task.

Test your newfound knowledge

1. How can the program break out of a `while` loop?

    a. Use a file hidden in a birthday cake.

    b. Make the `while` condition false.

    c. Call your friends for help.

    d. Use explosives.

2. How can a `while` loop run endlessly?

    a. Your computer goes crazy.

    b. The "nonstop" virus arrives.

    c. Your program never changes the `while` condition to false.

    d. The accelerator gets stuck.

Chapter 12

The foreach Loop

Say that you want to print the same letter to each of your friends inviting them to the big bash you're throwing because you just won the lottery. You want to personalize these invitations. You could write a program to print the text, but each time the program is run you find yourself entering the name of your next friend.

Of course, you avoid this problem by using the `foreach` loop. The `foreach` loop enables you to store all your friends' names in a list, and then your program uses each name when printing the invitation. It's like having a mail merge feature built into your own program.

So, whenever you want your programming code to execute a series of instructions as long as a condition is true, use the `while` loop. Your computer keeps executing instructions that you place inside a `while` loop until one of the instructions in your code changes the condition to false.

However, if you know how many times that you want the instructions to execute, use the `foreach` loop instead.

Just in case you can't wait, here's what a `foreach` loop looks like:

```
foreach VariableName (wordlist)
    Instruction
end
```

The wordlist is a list of string values that is assigned to the `VariableName`; I explain this wordlist stuff later in the chapter, so don't worry for now. (Remember that a string is any combination of letters and numbers.) The `VariableName` can be used by the instruction inside the `foreach` loop.

You can stuff as many instructions as you need inside the `foreach` loop. Your biggest challenge is your ability to keep track of the programming instructions that you enter. Use your common sense as a guide.

When to Use a `foreach` Loop

No hard-and-fast rules exist to tell you when to use a `foreach` loop. You just need to use your best judgment. (I guess you didn't have to go to MIT after all.)

Here are times when you can use a `foreach` loop:

- ✔ You need to do the same thing to more than one string value.
- ✔ You want to use a series of string values in a certain sequence.

For example, say that you want your program to give your five employees an increase in salary. Aren't you a nice person? The steps that are required to do this are as follows: Look up the employee's salary in the payroll file, calculate the new salary, and save the new salary to the payroll file.

You place the name of each employee in the list associated with the `foreach` loop. The program will then use the name of each employee in sequence to find the employee's record, perform the necessary math, and place the employee's record back into the file.

How the `foreach` Loop Works

Here's something to do when you're ready to show off your new programming talents to your friends. Write a program that greets each one of them personally when you have them gathered around your computer. You can do this in a couple of ways.

For example, you could type the following code:

```
echo "Hello, Mary."
echo "Hello, Joe."
echo "Hello, Sue."
```

This program simply has the same instruction repeated three times. Each time the name is changed to greet another one of your friends.

The following code also displays a Hello message to each of your three buddies:

```
@ counter = 1
while ($counter < 5)
   if ($counter == 1)then
        echo "Hello, Mary."
   endif
   if ($counter == 2)then
        echo "Hello, Joe."
   endif
   if ($counter == 3)then
        echo "Hello, Sue."
   endif
   @ counter = $counter + 1
end
```

Here's what is happening:

Each time instructions within the while loop are executed, the computer checks the value of @ counter.

Depending on the value of @ counter, a particular welcome message appears.

The last instruction in the while loop (@ counter = $counter + 1) tells the computer to add 1 to the value of $counter and then assign this new value to @ counter. This makes it possible for the computer to display all the messages.

After these instructions execute, the computer checks the value of $counter to see if the value is less than 5. If the value of $counter is less than 5, the instructions are executed another time. If the value of $counter is greater than 5, the loop ends.

The preceding program took 13 lines of code to accomplish the same result as the following foreach loop. I probably could have written in longhand in less time than it takes to simply read the code in the preceding example.

Here's how you can display a Hello greeting to each of your three pals using the foreach loop:

```
foreach friend (Mary Joe Sue)
echo "Hello, $friend ."
end
```

In the first line of the preceding foreach loop, you follow foreach friend with the names of your friends, placed within parentheses (Mary Joe Sue). This creates a wordlist (see the next section) and designates the names as values, which are then assigned to the variable $friend.

Did you notice the space between $friend and the following period? If you don't include this space, the program looks for a variable named friend. (with a period) and not friend (without a period).

Your computer takes the first value Mary and assigns it to $friend.

Then the greeting Hello, Mary. appears on the computer screen.

Your computer goes back and assigns the next value Joe to $friend.

This sequence continues until your computer runs out of values, in which case all of your friends have been greeted; then the loop ends.

So, you've cut down the amount of instructions that you need to type from the 13 lines using the while loop to three lines using the foreach loop. You've also made your program a lot easier to read by using the foreach loop.

Using a wordlist

The values that are assigned to the foreach variable are called the wordlist. A *wordlist* is a list of string values (a mixture of characters and numbers) that are sequentially assigned to a variable, one at a time.

By the way, a wordlist can be used with other statements besides the foreach loop. However, I think it's better to show here a routine when you typically use a wordlist.

Some points to remember about a wordlist:

- Values assigned to a wordlist must be a string value.
- Each value must be separated by a space.
- Place values within quotation marks if a space is part of the value.

Here's an example of how to use values that contain spaces:

```
foreach friend ("Mary Jones" "Joe Smith" "Sue Jones")
  echo "Hello, $friend ."
end
```

TECHNICAL STUFF

A foreach **loop is not a** for next **loop**

Some computer languages like Visual Basic have a for next loop, which lets you determine the number of times the instructions inside the loop are executed. UNIX C shell language does not have a for next loop. A few inexperienced UNIX programmers try to use the foreach loop as a replacement for a for next loop. This just won't work.

Here's a better way to control the number of times your computer executes instructions inside a loop: Use the while loop (refer to Chapter 11 for the lowdown on while loops). Take a look at this example:

```
@ counter = 1
while ($counter < 4)
    echo "This is my $counter time around."
    @ counter = $counter + 1
end
```

This program tells your computer to follow the instructions inside the loop three times. The last line increases the $counter variable by 1. The loop continues to run as long as the value of $counter is less than 4; the loop ends as soon as the value of $counter reaches 4.

You can control the number of times the computer executes instructions within the loop by changing the value of the condition of the while loop ($counter < 4).

Suppose that you want the program to execute the instructions ten times. Change the value 4 to the value 11. Changing the value to 11 means that the while loop continues as long as the value of $counter is less than 11.

Using a wordlist variable

There are a couple of ways to use a wordlist. As seen in the previous examples, names of your friends (values of the wordlist) can be used directly as part of the foreach loop. Another way is to assign your friends' names to a variable, and then use the variable with the foreach loop.

The following code shows how to assign a wordlist to a variable:

```
set names = (Mary Joe Sue)
foreach friend ($names)
  echo "Hello, $friend ."
end
```

In the preceding example of code, `set names = (Mary Joe Sue)` tells your program to create a wordlist variable called `names` and assign the variable the three values — `Mary`, `Joe`, and `Sue`.

In the second line of code, `foreach friend ($names)` tells your program to assign to the `friend` variable each value of the wordlist variable `$names`.

`echo "Hello, $friend ."` tells your program to display the greeting, such as `Hello, Mary.` or `Hello, Joe.`

`end` tells your program to end the `foreach` loop.

In essence, a wordlist lets you assign a whole list of values to a single variable that can be used in a `foreach` loop by using the name of the variable.

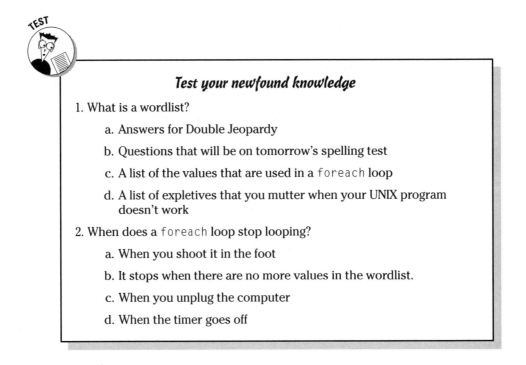

Test your newfound knowledge

1. What is a wordlist?

   a. Answers for Double Jeopardy

   b. Questions that will be on tomorrow's spelling test

   c. A list of the values that are used in a `foreach` loop

   d. A list of expletives that you mutter when your UNIX program doesn't work

2. When does a `foreach` loop stop looping?

   a. When you shoot it in the foot

   b. It stops when there are no more values in the wordlist.

   c. When you unplug the computer

   d. When the timer goes off

Chapter 13
Nested Loops and Quick Exits

*R*emember when Mom told you to clean up your toys? After complaining — which never did any good — you picked up the first toy and dropped it in the toy box. You repeated this action over and over again. However, among those toys were dozens of blocks, and each had to be placed in the canister that the blocks came in before the canister could be put into the toy box.

Picking up toys is the outside loop and picking up blocks is the inside loop. Loops can be jammed inside other loops to form an endless series of loops: *nested loops.* Nested loops make your program better organized — although a bit more complicated for you to read the program.

Using Nested Loops

A nested loop tells the program to do something a number of times (inside loop) for each time around the outside loop. I'll keep it simple and hold the explanation for later. The following block of code contains a nested loop:

```
@ flag = 1
while ($flag < 4)
    foreach friend (Bob Mary Sue)
    echo "Hello $friend ."
        end
        @ flag = $flag + 1
end
```

In brief, the program greets Bob, Mary, and Sue with a message on the screen three times. There are two loops in the program: the `while` loop and the `foreach` loop. The `while` loop goes around three times. The inner loop, which is the nested loop, displays the greeting to each friend every time the `while` loop goes around.

And now for the line-by-line details:

`@ flag = 1` says to create a numeric variable and assign the value 1 to it. (Don't worry; I explain `flag` later in this chapter.)

`while ($flag < 4)` says to check the value of the `@ flag` variable. If its value is 1, the program follows these instructions.

`foreach friend (Bob Mary Sue)` is the beginning of the nested loop. It says assign each of the values in the wordlist `(Bob Mary Sue)` to the variable `friend`.

`echo "Hello $friend ."` displays a greeting using the value of the `$friend` variable. (Notice the space between `$friend` and the period.)

`end` says this is the end of the `foreach` loop.

`@ flag = $flag + 1` assigns a 0 to the `@ flag` variable.

`end` indicates that this is the end of the `while` loop.

The `foreach` loop is the *inner loop*. The `while` loop is the *outer loop*. The inner loop must finish before the outer loop finishes.

Indenting Nested Loops

You can stuff as many loops as you need inside other loops. Your computer won't become confused. However, another programmer who may need to read your program may be confused by long blocks of code that contain lots of nested loops.

Avoid any confusion by indenting each inner loop. Indenting your nested loops makes your code easier to read and makes it easier to find where the loop begins and ends.

For example, take a look at the following code and note how difficult it is to pick out the nested loops:

```
@ flag = 1
while ($flag == 1)
foreach friend (Bob Mary Sue)
echo "Hello $friend ."
@ counter = 1
while ($counter < 4)
echo "$friend"
@ counter = $counter + 1
end
end
echo "Good-bye!"
@ flag = 0
end
```

Now, take a look at the same code in which nested loops are indented. Note that identifying the nested loops is much easier:

```
@ flag = 1
while ($flag == 1)
        foreach friend (Bob Mary Sue)
        echo "Hello $friend ."
        @ counter = 1
        while ($counter < 4)
                echo "$friend"
                @ counter = $counter + 1
        end
  end
  echo "Good-bye!"
  @ flag = 0
end
```

Indenting a nested loop has no effect on how UNIX processes the commands contained in the loop. The commands are processed in the same manner as in the block of code that is not indented — indenting a loop simply makes the code easier to read and easier to understand.

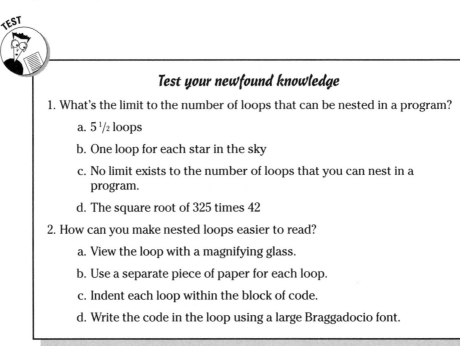

Test your newfound knowledge

1. What's the limit to the number of loops that can be nested in a program?

    a. 5 ½ loops

    b. One loop for each star in the sky

    c. No limit exists to the number of loops that you can nest in a program.

    d. The square root of 325 times 42

2. How can you make nested loops easier to read?

    a. View the loop with a magnifying glass.

    b. Use a separate piece of paper for each loop.

    c. Indent each loop within the block of code.

    d. Write the code in the loop using a large Braggadocio font.

Avoiding an Endless Loop

All right. You've built your masterpiece of a program filled with loops inside other loops (nested loops) but it doesn't work properly. The program keeps breaking out of an outer loop prematurely. It's a mess! This is a common mistake that you should avoid. Whenever code contains many nested loops, a good chance exists that changes made within an inner loop inadvertently makes the condition in an outer loop false — breaking your program out of the loop.

You can avoid this problem by making sure that the condition for each loop is independent from other conditions and other variables used in the program. It is common for programmers to use a variable called `flag` as the condition for a loop (for example, `while ($flag == 1)`). Inadvertently, the same flag can be used as the condition for all the nested loops. What a mess when the value of the flag variable changes. It potentially can affect the condition of all the loops. You'll end up with an endless loop — and then you'll have to untangle the mess.

Another common problem to avoid is ending the loop in the wrong place. Many programs have been tripped by this error, especially when loops are nested. Each loop requires its own `end` reserved words. If `end` is placed within the instructions of the loop instead of at the end of the instructions, the program will probably produce unexpected results. This problem is a little different from other problems that you face when you write a program because UNIX will not tell you that there's a mistake in your program. Instead, the program will execute as if nothing were wrong — except you'll recognize that the output of your program isn't correct. Only painstaking examination of your program will reveal the problem.

The following code shows a potential problem introduced by creating a nested loop:

```
@ flag = 1
while (@ flag == 1)
        foreach friend (Bob Mary Sue)
        echo "Hello $friend ."
        @ counter = 1
        while (@ counter < 4)
                echo "$friend"
                @ counter = @ counter + 1
                echo "Good-bye!"
                @ flag = 0
        end
    end
end
```

The end keywords are misplaced. Instead of displaying the Good-bye! message as part of the outer loop, the mix-up causes the Good-bye! message to be shown as part of the inner loop.

UNIX will not catch this mistake. You'll have to hunt through your code to locate the problem.

break *and* continue *Any Loop You Want*

I know that the following stuff on break and continue is connected with the while loop (which you can read about in Chapter 11, just in case you skipped it!), but I saved it for now because the topic usually comes up when you learn about nested loops and their potential problems. So don't stop now. Read on.

Using break for a quick exit

Did you ever try to run a mile on a treadmill just to call it quits halfway through? Practically the same thing can happen with your program when the program is executing a while loop. The treadmill has a safety button that you pull out to abort your run. The safety button in a while loop is the break reserved word.

A while loop runs continually until a condition is true or false. Suppose that you want to exit the loop before the condition changes. How can you bow out of the loop before it finishes? You can use the break statement.

Take a look at the following code for an example of the break statement in action:

```
set flag = "go"
while ($flag == "go")
  echo "Enter your name or type stop to end: "
  set friend = $<
  if ($friend == "stop")then
      break
  endif
  echo "Hello, $friend ."
end
echo "Good-bye!"
```

In this program, the user is asked to enter his or her name or the word stop if they want to end the program. Behind the scenes, the program displays a personal greeting on the screen as long as the word stop is not entered.

When stop is entered, the program enters the if statement and skips to the next instruction, which causes the program to break out of the loop. The break reserved word has practically the same effect as if the value of the flag variable is changed to something other than go — which would also cause the program to break out of the loop.

Finally, the program displays a farewell message on the screen.

Did you follow that? If not, I'll try another explanation. Here goes. The program is told to ask the user to enter a name; then the program displays a personalized greeting on the screen. When the user is finished, he or she types the word stop instead of a name. Each time a user enters a name, the program checks whether the word entered is stop. If the user enters the word stop, the program moves to the next line and executes the break statement, which ends the loop.

When your program is told to break, it immediately leaves the loop and continues to follow the instruction that comes after the end reserved word. In this example, your program displays the Good-bye! message.

continue *to the top of the loop*

Your computer does not have to follow all the instructions that you place inside a loop. Some instructions can be skipped if you use the continue statement. The following code demonstrates the use of the continue statement:

```
set flag = "go"
while ($flag == "go")
   echo "Enter your name or type stop to end: "
   set friend = $<
   if ($friend == "stop")then
        set flag = "stop"
        break
   endif
   if ($friend == "Tom")then
        continue
   endif
   echo "Hello, $friend ."
end
echo "Good-bye!"
```

Here's what's happening:

Your computer is told to ask the user to enter a name or enter the word stop to end the program. When the person enters his or her name, the program greets the person. However, when the word stop is entered, the program doesn't actually end. Instead, it resets the value of the flag variable, which causes the program to break out of the loop and jump to the last instruction in the program: Good-bye!

But Tom isn't your friend. So if Tom should enter his name, your computer won't greet him (I can't stand the guy, either). Instead, your computer is told to continue to the top of the loop.

The continue statement tells your program to skip the rest of the instructions within the loop and go directly to the top of the loop without displaying the greeting on the screen. When it gets there, the program checks the condition and decides whether or not to follow the instruction inside the loop again.

Part V
Writing
Subprograms

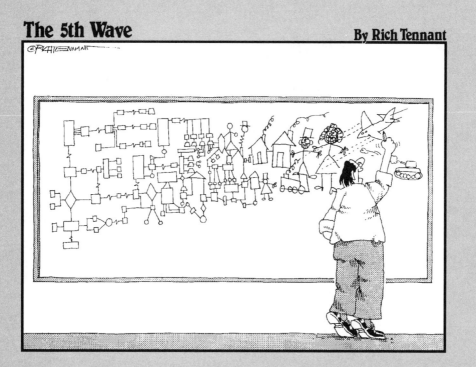

In this part . . .

*O*ne of the tricks to writing large, complex programs is to divide the program into smaller programs called subprograms. A *subprogram* performs one particular task of your program. Your job is to have your main program call the subprogram when needed. You discover how to use this trick with your own programs in this part.

Chapter 14

Subprograms
(That Everyone Can Share)

• •

• •

*A*lthough each program is designed to perform a specific task, every program that you write will have some basic functions in common. For example, every program displays text on a screen, reads information that a user enters on the keyboard, save the user's input information to a variable, and then does something with the information.

Each of these tasks are just pieces used to build large, complex programs that tell the computer to perform some useful tasks. There will be times when you want your program to perform a specific group of related tasks, such as displaying an error message on the screen when the user does something wrong with your program. Before you realize it, you'll be writing UNIX programs that enable your computer to do all sorts of fancy things.

Because these errors can occur practically anywhere in your program, it doesn't make sense to duplicate all the instructions necessary to display the error message throughout your program. This duplication takes up too much space and is a nightmare to maintain. Every time you want to change a part of the error message, you have to remember all the places in your program where you duplicated those instructions.

You can avoid the problems that are associated with duplicated instructions in your program by placing those instructions in a small program called a *subprogram*. A subprogram is identical to a regular program in that you create a subprogram using an editor and use the chmod command to transform the file into an executable program (a file that your computer can run).

The only thing special about a subprogram is that the instructions contained in a subprogram are designed to perform a *specific* task, such as displaying an error message on the screen or checking that the user's password is correct. Subprograms are then executed from within your program whenever you need a special task to be performed.

You'll find yourself building large, complex programs from many subprograms. However, to be sure that your program works smoothly and is also easy to read, the first step is mapping out the tasks you want your program to perform; then you decide how each task should relate to the other tasks in the program. This chapter takes you through the steps to create an overall program plan and how to use your program plan in creating subprograms.

Why Use a Subprogram?

Subprograms are the building blocks of your program. First, you create each building block, and then you assemble them to create the whole program.

Suppose that you need the computer to display an opening menu and respond to whatever the user selects. I call both of these activities one task because whenever a menu is displayed, the program always waits for a response from the user. All the code that is necessary to perform this task can be placed into the same subprogram. Your program then calls this subprogram whenever you want to perform this task.

Some reasons for using subprograms are as follows:

- ✔ Subprograms isolate all the code that performs a specific task. If you're having a problem with your menu display, for example, you don't have to hunt through your entire program for the piece of code that is causing a program. You just need to look in the "display menu" subprogram.

- ✔ Building your program from subprograms saves you from having to repeat the code elsewhere in your program. You simply execute the subprogram again and again from within your program anytime that you need the task performed.

- ✔ Changes or updates to code can be made in one place in your program.

- ✔ Subprograms are reusable and can be used to build other UNIX programs — and shared with other programmers who want their program to perform some of the same tasks that your program performs.

You need to use a little common sense when deciding on the number of subprograms you create for your program. If you find that you are losing track of the subprograms that you've created, chances are you've made too many of them (although there isn't any rule that tells you how many subprograms are too many). When you feel that tracking subprograms are getting out of control, it's time to consolidate them or come up with a better planning tool to help you organize you subprograms. Probably the best planning tool is the flow chart graphically depicting your program plan.

Creating a Program Plan with a Flowchart

Just the mention of creating a UNIX program plan can send most new programmers off to get a bottle of aspirin. Why must computers be so complicated? I thought that I'd never be able to learn Microsoft Project (a tool that many programming gurus love to use when building a plan), but with a little patience I was able to overcome this perceived obstacle. You too will find creating a UNIX program plan daunting at first, but it's really pretty easy.

You are going to first figure out what you want the UNIX program to do, and then break down the overall plan into individual functions. Using a flow chart helps you plot your plan.

Divide and conquer

How do you eat an elephant? One bite at a time, of course. How then do you plan a large, complex UNIX program? You break the program down by its individual functions and create a list of what you want your UNIX program to do. (You can also chomp on the program, but you'll find it rather stringy and in need of garlic.) By dividing your UNIX program into logical chunks, each of which performs a unique and important task, you make your overall programming task much easier.

For example, suppose that you want to create a UNIX program that has the overall objective of maintaining your telephone directory. This overall program objective can be further divided into the individual tasks that the program should perform, which may include some of the following:

- ✔ Logging in to the program
- ✔ Displaying a main menu that lets the user make a selection
- ✔ Finding a listing in the telephone directory
- ✔ Adding a listing to the telephone directory
- ✔ Modifying a listing in the telephone directory
- ✔ Printing the telephone directory

Your UNIX program may have more or fewer tasks than appear in the preceding list. However, almost all programs that work with data have subprograms that find data, add data, modify existing data, and print data.

Plugging a task list into a flowchart

Now it's time to take pencil in hand and organize your thoughts about how your program is going to work. The simplest approach is to draw a flow chart where each box in the flow chart represents a task that your program must accomplish. Each box on the flow chart must be arranged in the order the task is to be accomplished by your program, and then you can draw lines connecting the boxes.

Take an example close to my heart (actually close to my stomach). I call this the Get a Snack program. Here's how I organized this nightly trip (now if I could only get my computer to do the fetching I'd have it made).

For example, a flowchart for the "Get a Snack program" may look something like the chart in Figure 14-1.

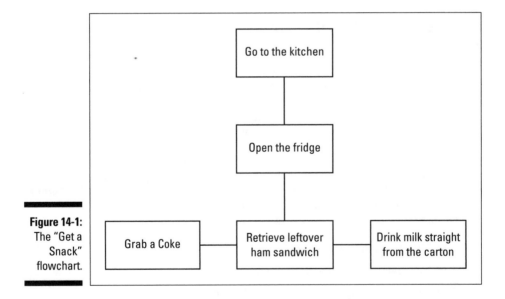

Figure 14-1: The "Get a Snack" flowchart.

Get started, then, with your program flowchart. After you assemble the long list of tasks that you want your UNIX program to perform, the next step is to draw a picture of your program. All you need is a box for each task; then place the name of the task inside the box like that in Figure 14-2 — just like I did with the "Get a Snack" program, but this time starting from the very beginning.

Figure 14-2:
The
beginnings
of a fine
flowchart.

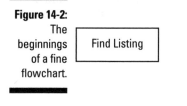

This doesn't add much to your plan. But this is just the first step. The next step in creating a flowchart is to map out how each task is related to the other tasks. Now this is getting a little complicated, isn't it?

The flowchart in Figure 14-3 shows how the UNIX user progresses through your program. The user first logs in (Login Task), and the main menu appears (Display Menu). From the main menu, the user can then select one of the four options you provide in the program — Find Listing, Add Listing, Modify Listing, or Print Listing.

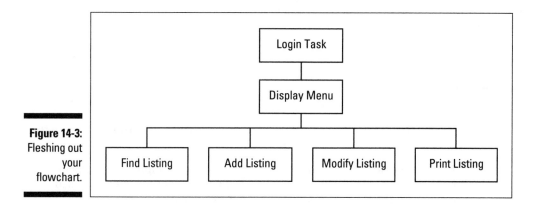

Figure 14-3:
Fleshing out
your
flowchart.

Adding detail to a flowchart

Each task shown on your flowchart can be further divided into more specific tasks. For example, the task of "Find Listing" requires these more detailed tasks to be performed by your program:

- ✔ Prompt the user to enter a name to find
- ✔ Search the database for the name the user entered
- ✔ If the search is successful, display the listing
- ✔ If the search is unsuccessful, tell the user that the listing wasn't found
- ✔ Return to the main menu

Draw another flowchart that shows each of these more detailed tasks and how each task logically follows from the preceding one. Figure 14-4 shows how the Find Listing flowchart should look.

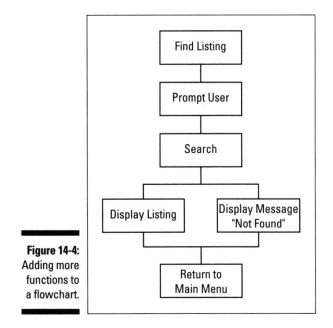

Figure 14-4:
Adding more functions to a flowchart.

The shape of Figure 14-4 is a little different than Figure 14-3. This is because the relationships among the tasks are now different.

As you become more specific about what each task (subprogram) does in your UNIX program, the flowchart that depicts that task also gets more detailed — kind of like branches sprouting from the trunk of a healthy tree.

Linking subprograms in a flowchart

As you map out more and more tasks on your UNIX program flowchart, it may become tough to keep track of all those subprograms. By numbering a subprogram, as shown in Figure 14-5, you can make reference to another flow chart that contains more details about that subprogram.

Suppose that you're building a program that requires a user to enter his or her name and password into the program before using the program. So, the first box on the flow chart is labeled "Login Task." This tells you generally what takes place at this portion of your program.

Arrow your flowcharts

You can dress up your drawings by placing arrows on the lines that connect tasks. The arrows show the direction of the next task. These are not required, although they add clarity to your drawing.

Each box in the flow chart is a task which is associated with other boxes (tasks) on your flow chart by a connecting line. The line does more than join boxes. The line shows how each box is related to another box by using an arrow at the end of the line. For example, the task of displaying the menu comes before the user enters one of the selections from the menu. So, you'll have a line connecting the first box (displaying the menu) to the second box (selecting from the menu) with an arrow pointing to the second set of box because this task comes after the first task.

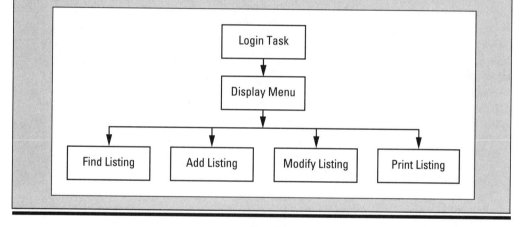

But what's involved in the Login Task? You need to know this information when you build the subprogram that handles the login task. However, there isn't room in the "Login Task" box to place all these details.

Here's the solution. Number each box on your flow chart. The first box is 1, the second is 2; you get the idea. If a box needs more detail, create a separate flow chart for that box. In this way you have plenty of room on the second flow chart to identify all the tasks that are associated with the box on the previous flow chart.

Suppose that the "Login Task" on the first flow chart is assigned number 1. You then create a whole new flow chart just for the "Login Task." The first box on the Login Flow chart is number 1.0, and this box has the same text as the text used on the corresponding box on the first flow chart — "Login Task."

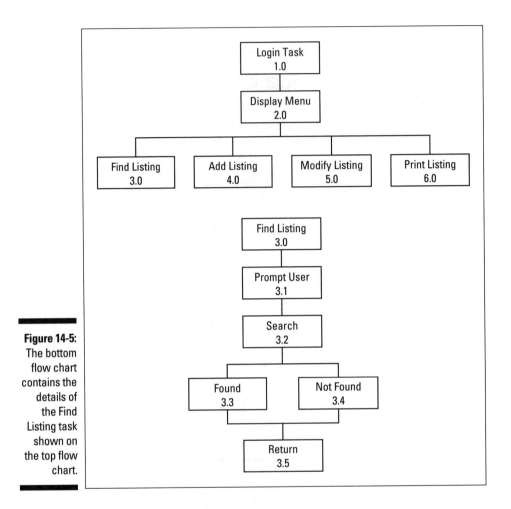

Figure 14-5:
The bottom
flow chart
contains the
details of
the Find
Listing task
shown on
the top flow
chart.

Create boxes on the "Login Task" flow chart, using the steps shown in the previous section, to represent all the tasks that are necessary for the user to log into the program. Each box on the "Login Task" flow chart must also be numbered. However, instead of numbering the boxes as 1, 2, 3, and so on, you number them as 1.1, 1.2, 1.3, and so on. This numbering method lets you quickly know that the box you are looking at is associated with a box on the first flow chart. The first number (1) is the number of the box related box on the first flow chart. The second number (.1) is the number of the box on the second flow chart.

The technical name for associating boxes on one flow chart to another flow chart is a *leveling diagram.* The first flow chart is level one and the second flow chart is level two. And there can be level three, level four, and so on as needed.

Using a Flowchart to Create UNIX Subprograms

After you map out your UNIX program on a flow chart and have numbered each box appropriately, the next step is to write the programming code for each task. Each module or box on the flow chart represents a distinct function or task for which you write code.

You have to decide whether or not the code for a task should be included directly in your program or in a subprogram. Here is the criterion to use when making this decision: A task that requires little or no help from the program or from a subprogram and is repeatedly used in the program is a good candidate to become a subprogram.

How to create a subprogram

You create a subprogram in the same way that you create a program. The flow chart that you created shows you all the steps that you must include in the subprogram. Your job is to translate these steps into UNIX programming instructions. (See Chapter 2).

After you determine the instructions that you need to have the program carry out the task, you type those instructions into a text file using a text editor such as vi. (I introduce vi in Chapter 3; refer also to Appendix B for vi details.) Then save the file to your hard disk. Make the file an executable file by using the chmod command (refer to Chapter 1) and execute your new subprogram from the command prompt. This process lets you test you subprogram before your use the subprogram in your program.

Some rules for writing subprograms are as follows:

- ✔ Instructions must appear in the subprogram in the order in which you want the program to perform those instructions.
- ✔ Each subprogram must be saved in its own file.
- ✔ Each subprogram file must be converted into an executable file using the chmod command.
- ✔ Each subprogram should be run at the command line to be sure that it runs smoothly. If not, you must debug the subprogram until all the problems are resolved.

Say that you want to create a program that manages your personal telephone directory. The program has these tasks:

- ✔ Display a menu
- ✔ Read the user's selection
- ✔ Determine the selection made by the user
- ✔ Find a telephone listing
- ✔ Add a new telephone listing to the file
- ✔ Modify an existing telephone list in the file
- ✔ Quit the program
- ✔ Print a telephone listing

It makes sense that the first three tasks are placed in the program itself because these are the central functions of the program. The task of quitting the program too is made part of the program. The other tasks are built into subprograms because these tasks are a relatively self-contained piece of the program. For example, you don't really need the menu to find a telephone listing. You could simply run a subprogram that takes care of this task.

Each subprogram is given a name that identifies the task that the subprogram performs. The findlisting subprogram, for example, finds a telephone listing in the file. After this subprogram is built, you can run it from the command line — independent from the program. All the instructions to ask the user for the name of the person whose telephone number they want to see and the instructions to locate and display the telephone number on the screen are all contained in the findlisting subprogram.

After you determine that each of these subprograms runs smoothly, you can make the names of the subprograms part of your program. When your program sees the name of a subprogram, your program executes the subprogram just as you did at the command line. This is also referred to as *calling the subprogram* from your program. Here's how it looks:

```
clear
echo "Telephone Directory"
echo " "
echo "1. Find Listing"
echo "2. Add Listing"
echo "3. Modify Listing"
echo "4. Print Listing"
echo "Q. Quit"
echo " "
set selection = $<
switch ($selection)
   case "1":
```

```
      findlisting
      breaksw
   case "2":
      addlisting
      breaksw
   case "3":
      modifylisting
      breaksw
   case "4":
      printlisting
      breaksw
       case "Q":
    exit
endsw
```

When the user makes a selection, the program determines if it needs to run a particular subprogram to complete the task that is requested by the user. If so, the name of the subprogram is called and instructions contained in the subprogram take over. After the task is completed, the subprogram ends and the program retakes control by executing the next instruction in the program.

Choosing a name for a subprogram

A subprogram's name is important to a programmer. The subprogram's name helps the programmer recognize the subprogram and can be used to identify the purpose of the subprogram. For example, you could name a subprogram something short and easy like sub1. But then try to remember what the sub1 subprogram does when you are rushing about writing your code. (Now let's see, was sub1 the Login Task subprogram or is it the subprogram to print a name list?)

For example, I call the sample subprogram in the preceding section displaymenu. This subprogram name briefly describes what the subprogram does — it *displays the menu*. displaymenu is also an easy name to remember.

Keep the following points in mind when you name your subprograms:

- ✔ The subprogram name should be informative. For example, although the name displaymenu appears to meet this requirement, displaymenu doesn't mention which menu is being displayed.

- ✔ Use abbreviations in the subprogram name. You can rename the displaymenu subprogram to something like dispopenmu, which implies *disp*lay *open*ing *menu*. Make sure that the meaning of the abbreviations are easily recognizable.

Test your newfound knowledge

1. What's the first step in writing a complex UNIX program?

    a. Call your local computer company for help.

    b. Hit your head against the wall repeatedly (which always feels better when you stop).

    c. Draw a flowchart of the program before writing your code.

    d. Buy a satellite navigation system.

2. Why are subprograms helpful?

    a. They go underwater for long periods of time.

    b. Subprograms fit better inside your computer.

    c. Little guys are easier to control.

    d. Subprograms reduce a large, complex UNIX program into smaller, manageable modules.

✔ Try to reflect the name of the main program in the name of the subprogram. For example, the name `dispopenmu` states that this subprogram *dis*plays the *open* *menu* — but the opening menu for which program? To make this subprogram name more informative, you could rename this subprogram to add the name of the main program — `tddispopenmu` to imply *t*elephone *d*irectory *dis*play *open*ing *menu*.

✔ The subprogram name must be easy to read — you can play around with the capitalization to make it easier to read. For example, the name `tddispopenmu` identifies the subprogram, but it's hard to read. This is better `TdDispOpenMu`.

Keep in mind that there is no hard and fast rule that will show you how to properly name a subprogram. However, you can stay out of trouble by using your common sense.

How to use a subprogram

After your program plan is complete, it's time for you to decide which tasks are to be included in your program and which tasks are to be built as a bunch of subprograms.

Test your subprogram, and then create your program. Some programmers call this the *main program* because this is the starting point for your program. As you create your program, place the name of the appropriate subprogram into the program wherever you want the subprogram's task performed in your program.

The name of the subprogram is inserted as an instruction into your program the same way as you place the other instructions into your program. In fact, you could write a program that has one instruction in the name of a subprogram. Here's what this program looks like.

```
#!/bin/csh
displaymenu
```

There's not much to this program. It simply starts the C shell and then calls the displaymenu subprogram. The subprogram does all the work, in this case. The displaymenu subprogram displays a menu on the screen.

You can build large, complex programs from many subprograms. And sometimes subprograms can be reused in other programs without having to modify the subprogram. For example, a subprogram prompting the user to enter a name and password and then validating the password can be used with other programs that need this task.

Sharing Subprograms

Don't throw away the subprograms that you build! Programmers treat their collection of subprograms almost as collector's items. A subprogram that is working smoothly is worth its weight in gold. Okay, maybe it's not that valuable yet. But a programmer who has the choice of building a subprogram from scratch or getting one from a friend will always opt for the trade.

Don't go looking for a formal trading post where subprograms are exchange. There really isn't any. However, you can post your request for subprograms on the appropriate newsgroups on the Internet or on CompuServe (see Chapter 20 for details). You can also ask other programmers that you meet if they have any good subprograms that you can take a peek at.

Chapter 15

Passing and Accepting Arguments

● ●

In This Chapter

▶ Arguments, arguments, arguments

▶ Passing arguments

▶ Accepting arguments

▶ Avoiding problems with arguments

▶ Checking to see if your argument really exists

● ●

*H*ey, here's a good one to use the next time you want to argue with your significant other. Just say, "I'm not arguing; I'm simply passing you information." Feel free to use this expression (but don't attribute it to me).

Most of us think of an argument as words of disagreement that can heat up and sometimes lead to blows. But to your computer, an argument is information that is sent to a program (or a subprogram) from the command line when the program (or subprogram) is executed.

The transfer of the information from the command line to the program (or subprogram) is commonly referred to as *passing arguments*. (The information that is passed resides outside the program or subprogram that is going to use the information.)

Say that you want to run the subprogram that finds a listing in your personal telephone directory. We'll call this subprogram findlisting and assume that the subprogram doesn't prompt you to enter the person's name that you are trying to locate. Instead, you pass the name of the person as an argument to the program. Here's how you would enter the information at the command line:

```
findlisting Jones
```

The name *Jones* is automatically passed to the findlisting subprogram by the UNIX operating system. The findlisting subprogram then uses the name to search for Jones's telephone number. After the number is found, the findlisting subprogram displays the number on the screen — if the programmer has provided the subprogram the necessary instructions.

Why Use Arguments?

The capability to pass arguments is an important feature of UNIX because this feature enables you to build flexible programs and subprograms. Remember, a program can really be a group of subprograms. Each subprogram performs one task very well. After a subprogram is built and running smoothly, you probably won't need to modify the instructions within the subprogram. (If it ain't broken, leave it alone.)

Although you don't want to fool around with the "innards" of a subprogram, you do want the subprogram to use the information that pertains to your current program. And the best way to do this is to pass the information to the subprogram as an argument on the command line.

Say that you built a subprogram to fetch you snacks from the kitchen (just dreaming). The subprogram is all ready to do the legwork for you. However, the subprogram needs to know what snacks you want. How can you do this? Well, when you call the subprogram, you pass the name of the snack on the command line. If the subprogram was written to receive the snack information, you could sit back in your recliner and keep surfing the tube.

Although I've been saying that arguments are passed on the command line to the program or subprogram, you can also pass arguments from within your program using the name of the program followed by the argument.

Passing an argument to a program (or subprogram) is different from what you've seen in earlier chapters. In all the programs that you've created so far, the information that is needed for your program is always provided to your program as *values* assigned to *variables*. With some programs, information is placed inside your program as part of the code, as in this line of code:

```
set FirstName = "Bob"
```

In the preceding line of code, the name Bob is assigned to the string variable FirstName. This is called *hard coding* the information into the program. Hard coding is a term used by programmers to say that the information is typed directly into the program. Every time you want to change the data, you must change the program.

You have also seen another way that a program gathers information that it needs: A program can ask the user to enter the information while the program is running:

```
set FirstName
echo "Enter your first name: "
FirstName $<
```

Here, the user is asked to enter his or her first name. The name is then assigned by the program to the string variable FirstName. The information entered by the user changes every time the program runs without the programmer having to change anything inside the program.

Hard coding information is not always the best way to get information into your program because the programmer needs to change the program each time the information changes.

Asking the user to enter the information each time the program runs is better than hard coding the information into the program. However, there are times when the user is unable to provide the necessary information. For example, say you've written a program to send out an invitation to your big promotion bash to everyone whose name appears in your personal telephone directory — but you don't want to enter each name individually. So, you sit down to write a UNIX program to do the work for you.

You follow all the tips that I've given you and create a subprogram that prints the invitation. However, each time this subprogram prints, it needs one name from your telephone directory. Of course, you don't expect the subprogram to prompt you to enter each name. Instead, your program recalls each name from your telephone directory and passes the name as an argument when the program calls the subprogram.

Passing Arguments

You start your program by entering the name of your program on the command line:

```
% displaymenu
```

The % sign is the command prompt for the C shell. This prompt is already on your screen. (Although I don't usually show you the prompt in this book, I need to use it in this section to set up the example.)The name of the program that is being called by UNIX is displaymenu. You can send data to the program by placing the data to the right of the name of the program.

```
% displaymenu yes
```

The word `yes` is the information that is being sent to the program `displaymenu`.

You can also pass information to a subprogram. You call a subprogram from within a program or from another subprogram using the following command:

```
displaymenu
```

Notice the % sign is missing. This is because the program is being called from within another program. The % sign is only there when you start the program from the command line.

You can send data to a subprogram in the same way as you send data to a program from the command line:

```
displaymenu yes
```

Here are some rules to follow when sending data to a program from the command line:

- ✔ Place a space between the name of the program and the data.
- ✔ Place a space between each data item when multiple data is sent to the program. See the upcoming "Passing Multiple Arguments" section for more lowdown on multiple data.

Accepting Arguments

Well, if your program (or subprogram) can be passed information, you'd better write instructions in your program (or subprogram) to do something with the information when it is received. This activity is commonly referred to as *accepting arguments*.

The information that is passed to your program is stored by UNIX in a variable called `$agrv`, and you use `[1]` (that's a number 1 placed within brackets) because the number 1 tells your program that you want to refer to the first piece of information that is passed to the program. (As you'll see later in this chapter, more than one piece of information can be passed to the program.) For example

```
$agrv[1]
```

If your program is the one that's getting you a snack from the kitchen, this is like telling it what kind of snack you want. You write something like this:

```
getsnack chips
```

The program sees chips as the value that is assigned to the $agrv[1]$ variable. The program just goes about its business using $agrv[1]$ whenever it needs to refer to the snack that you want from the kitchen.

Now, let's get real and take a look at a practical way of using this. In the next example, I do something sneaky. I create a displaymenu program that displays a menu, receives a response from the user, and then executes the appropriate subprogram. However, this program displays the menu and does all the other stuff only if the magic word — *yes* — is passed to the program. Otherwise the program skips directly to the end of the program without showing anything on the screen.

Your program can do more than just display the data item it receives. Sometimes the data is used as the criteria for your computer to make a decision.

Here's how I do the displaymenu program that I just mentioned:

```csh
#!/bin/csh
if ($argv[1] == "yes") then
   clear
   echo "Telephone Directory"
   echo " "
   echo "1. Find Listing"
   echo "2. Add Listing"
   echo "3. Modify Listing"
   echo "4. Print Listing"
   echo "Q. Quit"
   echo " "
   set selection = $<
   switch ($selection)
           case "1":
           findlisting
              breaksw
           case "2":
              addlisting
              breaksw
           case "3":
              modifylisting
              breaksw
           case "4":
              printlisting
              breaksw
           case "Q":
              exit
      endsw
endif
```

This is an involved version of the displaymenu program because the program is receiving information from the command line. The menu is displayed only if the user sent the program a magic word. The magic word is yes. Here's what happens in a nutshell:

1. The computer starts the C shell.

2. The data sent to the program is compared to the word yes.

3. If the data and the magic word match, the menu is displayed and the computer does something when a selection is made by the user.

4. If the data and the magic word don't match, the program ends.

Passing Multiple Arguments

A program can pass your program (or subprogram) more than one argument from the command line. This capability becomes very useful whenever your program requires more than one piece of information to perform a task.

Say that you've written a program that displays names on the screen — names of your friends. If the program is written to accept these names from the command line, you can place each name on the command line, making sure each one is separated by a space. Your program recognizes where one piece of information begins and the other ends by the space character. Take a glance at this:

```
displayfriends Bob Mary Joe Sue
```

Each piece of information must appear to the right of the program name. A space must separate each data item.

Your program can use this information by using the $agrv variable (explained in the preceding section) with the corresponding number of the data item. For example

```
#!/bin/csh
echo "My friend $argv[1]"
echo "My friend $argv[2]"
echo "My friend $argv[3]"
echo "My friend $argv[4]"
```

This program shows the names of your friends on the screen:

```
My friend Bob
My friend Mary
My friend Joe
My friend Sue
```

Learning how to pass multiple arguments to your program and subprograms provides flexibility to your programming. You no longer have to write all the information that your program requires into the code. Nor do you have to constantly prompt the user for information. Instead, you can simply enter the information on the command line or when your program calls a subprogram, and the information is passed to the program or subprogram.

Problems with Sending Arguments

Two common problems can occur whenever your program or subprogram is sent arguments: Someone can send you the wrong number of arguments or the wrong kind of arguments.

The wrong number of arguments

You can plan to receive a fixed number of arguments, but nothing forces someone to send you the correct number. Suppose your program expects two arguments:

```
#!/bin/csh
echo "First Name: $agrv[1]"
echo "Last Name: $agrv[2]"
```

And someone supplies only one of those arguments:

```
displayname Bob
```

Your program is still telling your computer to use the second data item that is passed to the program, the phantom data.

The wrong kind of argument

Your program depends on someone else to pass it the correct information. If this person is not dependable, your program has problems. Say that someone called your program and sent this information:

```
namegame car truck
```

And your program assumes that the information is just what it is looking for.

```
#!/bin/csh
echo "First Name: $agrv[1]"
echo "Last Name: $agrv[2]"
```

But it isn't. Who is going to be blamed for the problem? The person using your program or the programmer? (Who, you? It's not your fault.) There isn't an easy way that you can avoid this situation or the blame (except by not answering the phone when the user calls to complain). As long as you have made note in the documentation of your program that the user needs to enter specific kinds of information at the command prompt when the program runs, your job is done. You can't be expected to force the user to read the documentation before running your program. But you'll still hear: "OF COURSE I . . . didn't . . . READ THE INSTRUCTIONS."

Does Your Argument Exist?

Your program sometimes needs to have data sent to it, otherwise your program can't perform the task. So the first thing your program needs to do is to determine if any data was sent to it.

You can use the $#argv variable to determine the number of data items received by your program. The $#argv variable contains the number of arguments that is passed to your program. Notice there is a difference between $argv, which is used to reference an argument, and $#argv, which just contains the number of arguments that your program received.

Here's how you do it:

```
#!/bin/csh
echo "$#agrv"
```

This program displays the number of data items it received. When you run this program, you won't see the data itself; instead you'll see a number on the screen.

You can compare the value of $#agrv with the number of data items that your program requires.

```
#!/bin/csh
if ($#argv == 2)then
  echo "You entered the correct number of arguments."
else
  echo "You didn't enter the correct number of arguments."
endif
```

In the preceding code, the program starts the C shell, and then it determines if the correct number of arguments was passed to the program. In this case, I decided that two arguments are necessary based upon the specifications for the program. This example is only the beginning of the program.

So, the program uses the if statement to compare the value in $#argv with the value 2. If there is a match, the program displays a message and continues (although the rest of the program isn't shown). If there isn't a match, the program ends.

You can also determine if no arguments were entered by writing something like this in your program:

```
#!/bin/csh
if ($#argv < 1)then
  echo "You didn't enter the correct number of arguments."
endif
```

This program checks to determine if the value of $#argv is less than 1 — meaning that no arguments were entered on the command line. If this is the case, a message is displayed: You didn't enter the correct number of arguments. And although the instructions aren't shown, you would probably end the program if no information is passed from the command line.

Test your newfound knowledge

1. How can your program access the first argument it receives from the command line?

    a. By calling my mother-in-law. She has access to everything.

    b. A heavy-duty tire iron will do.

    c. By referencing the `$argv[1]` variable

    d. By calling Louis Freeh, the FBI chief

2. How can you be sure that your program receives the proper number of arguments?

    a. Don't worry. No one would dare to send less than the required number.

    b. Check the value of the `$#agrv` variable.

    c. Get your program a subscription to *Argument Digest*.

    d. Check the whatchamacallit chip in your computer.

Part VI
Database Programs and Printing

In this part . . .

*I*nformation that your program gathers from someone who uses it is usually saved in a file for later use or is printed on paper. In this part, you find out how to save information to a file as a database. You also discover how to find a particular piece of information stored in a file. Finally, you learn how to print information on paper. What more could you ask for?

Chapter 16

Using Database Files

● ●

In This Chapter

▶ Creating a database file

▶ Saving information to a database file

▶ Finding information in a database file

● ●

May I have the file on Jones? Sure can. And with a few strokes of the keyboard, up comes the information about Jones on-screen. It's a miracle. Those mystical computers get the needed data in seconds and without making a mistake (ha).

Very little magic is involved in how a computer locates all the information that you thought was confidential. You, too, can perform this trick by following a few simple steps:

✔ Decide what information you want to store and retrieve.

✔ Plan how you want your computer to store the information.

✔ Learn the proper words to use to ask your computer to find the information that you want.

What Is Data?

Information is a bunch of words that has some meaning to us. For example, we recognize the letter *B* as a letter of the alphabet that represents the phonetic sound *ba*. If we combine the letter *B* with two more letters, *ob,* we come up with a different meaning for the letter *B*. Now it's part of the word *Bob*.

Combine the word *Bob* with the numbers *555-55-5555* (which looks a lot like a Social Security number). This data then identifies a specific individual whose first name is Bob. By combining letters into words and words into meaningful data, we form information that we can use to manage our affairs.

Keep in mind that this data is only meaningful to us. To the computer, it looks very confusing — that is, until the letters are translated into something your computer understands: a series of zeros and ones.

What Is a File?

Words that you type at the prompt using your keyboard are displayed on-screen by your computer. You can read the data, but you can't do much else with it.

To make the information useful, you need to save it to a file. A *file* is a place on the computer's hard drive (or floppy disk) where data is stored; the data stays there when you turn off your computer. Think of a file as a folder that you place in a file drawer. The drawer, in this case, is the computer's hard drive.

Saving information to a file

The most simple way to save information to a file is to use the echo reserved word. Here's how you do this:

```
echo "Bobbie" > friends
```

This tells the computer to take the word Bobbie and, instead of showing it on the screen, put it into a file called friends.

Notice that the greater-than operator (>) is used. This is called the *redirection* operator. It tells the computer to change the place where it normally shows data, which is the screen. (Nerds call this redirecting the *output* from standard *out* to the disk.)

Be careful when you save information to a file using the redirection operator. If the file already exists, the information that is stored in the file is replaced with new information.

Appending information to a file

No one wants to overwrite information each time that new information is saved to a file. A better way is to place the new information at the end of the existing information. This is called *appending* information to a file.

```
echo "Bobbie" >> friends
```

You use two greater-than signs ($>>$) to tell the computer to put the information at the end of the file. If the file does not exist, the computer creates a new file and places the information into the file.

Displaying information that is stored in a file

After the information is saved to a file, you can turn off your computer and go do something exciting. When you come back, you find that the information still resides on the hard drive. You can show the information that you saved to a file by using the `cat` utility.

```
cat friends
```

This tells the computer to copy each character in the file named `friends` and display these characters on the screen. (The whiz kids called this *concatenating* the information that is stored in the file to standard out — which is the screen.)

Information that is shown on the screen is a copy of the information that is stored in the file. The original information remains in the file until you overwrite or append the file.

A File and a Database

Some programmers confuse a file with a database. This is easy to do, because a database is a kind of file. Information that is stored in a database is stored in a file on a disk. But not all information that is stored in a file is stored in a database. You knew I was going to say that, right?

A file has these characteristics:

- ✔ Contains information in no particular order
- ✔ Is not organized in a way to find the information quickly
- ✔ Can have mixed kinds of information

A database, however, has these traits:

- ✔ Contains information in a particular order
- ✔ Is organized in a way to find the information quickly
- ✔ Has a unique kind of information

Think of a database as way to organize information that is in your file folder. Placing information in a file folder is like storing information in a file. Organizing that information in the file folder so that you can quickly find what you are looking for is like storing information in a database.

Databases and Database Management Systems

When most programmers talk about a database, they are really talking about a database management system. A *database management system* is a group of programs that works together to create and maintain a database file.

You can purchase many popular database management systems for your computer. However, they are expensive and often found on large commercial computer systems. With a bit of effort, you can create your own database management system.

A word of caution: Don't expect your system to manage any important data. You need a commercial database management system for any serious database jobs. Your system is perfect to work with small amounts of data and to learn how a database system works.

Creating a Database

The first step in creating a database is to decide how you are going to organize your information. You must ask yourself what information should be stored in the database. Consider storing the information that is contained in a telephone directory (the electronic version of your black book). Make a list of the things that are normally found:

- ✔ First name
- ✔ Last name
- ✔ Telephone number

Columns and rows

This list defines the rows and columns of the database. A *row* is a horizontal line that contains a set of data (called a *record*). For example, all the information about Bob Smith is contained on the same line. Each person has his or her own line in the database.

A *column* is a group of the same kind of data (called a *field*). For example, all the first names are in the same column, as are all of the last names.

The data looks like this:

```
Bob Smith   555-1212
Mary Jones  555-5555
Tom Adams   555-7777
```

Notice that each line contains the same kind of information in the same order (first name, last name, telephone number). This is why the data forms a database.

Here's the same information that isn't in a database format:

```
555-1212 Bob Smith
Mary Jones 555-5555
Adams, Tom, 555-7777
```

Information about each person is on its own line, which is fine for a database. However, the columns don't contain similar information. The data is simply unorganized.

Saving information to a database

Although a file is not always a database, a database *is* a file. (Am I confusing you?) You save information to a database the same way that you save information to a file. Here's how you do it:

```
echo "Bob Smith 555-1212" >> friends
echo "Mary Jones 555-5555" >> friends
echo "Tom Adams 555-7777" >> friends
```

The first line tells the computer to save information about Bob to the file called friends. If the file doesn't exist, the computer creates this file.

The second line tells the computer to save information about Mary to the end of the file called friends.

The last line tells the computer to save the information about Tom to the end of the same file.

Finding Information in a Database with vi

The kind of file that you use as the database file is called a *text file*. This file is almost like the file that you create using your word processor — except that all the instructions for those fancy features (for example, font size) are removed. When you want to find information in the file, your computer must search each line in the database file.

Start vi

A number of methods can be used to locate data in your database file. The easiest and yet most time-consuming method is to use a text editor, such as vi. (See Appendix B for all the details you want to know about vi.) Try the following at the command prompt:

```
vi friends
```

Press Enter, and a page of the database file is shown on the screen (assuming, of course, that you have a file named friends).

Search methods with vi

You can then use two methods to find information:

- ✔ The hunt-and-peck method. You hunt through each page on the screen and then peck at the PgDn key to bring up another page.
- ✔ The find feature of vi. Ask the program to locate the data for you.

These, of course, are not the best ways to search for information in the database file. A much better method is to use a UNIX utility, which is a program that is designed to search your database.

Finding Information in a Database with awk

The awk utility is one of the most popular tools that programmers use to search a database file. It has two parts:

- ✔ A search pattern
- ✔ Data that you want to be displayed

Here's how you use this command:

```
awk '/Smith/ {print $1, $2, $3}'friends
```

This command tells your computer to look for the character Smith in the database file friends. Then the computer displays the first, second, and third column of all rows that match Smith. Notice the use of the curly brackets ({}) and the single quote marks with the awk command.

Create the search expression

The information that you are looking for in the database file is called the search expression. The *search expression* tells the computer how to identify the rows in your database that you want to see.

The search expression must

- ✔ Appear at the beginning of the awk command line
- ✔ Be placed with the forward slash character (/)

Building a search expression for the awk utility can become complex because it is a very powerful utility. If you really want to dig into building complex search expressions, use the man pages to see the online documentation. The man command displays the manual pages relating to a particular UNIX utility or command. Here's how you issue the command at the UNIX prompt:

```
man awk
```

Match characters

The simplest search expression tells the computer to find an exact match of a pattern. The *pattern* contains the characters that appear somewhere in the database file.

Perhaps you want to see all of the rows from the friends database file that have 555 as the first three digits of the telephone number. The pattern that you want to match is 555-.

Notice that the hyphen (-) is placed at the end of the pattern. This is because the first three digits of the telephone number end with a hyphen, at least in your database file. If the hyphen is omitted from the search expression, any occurrence of 555 in a row is selected by the computer.

Here's how the search expression looks:

```
awk '/555-/ {print $1, $2, $3}'friends
```

This results in the computer displaying all of the rows in the `friends` database file, because each telephone number begins with `555`.

Watch out for spaces

Whenever you tell the computer to find an exact match in a database file, you must consider that spaces separating columns can be a required part of the search expression.

Consider adding the name `John Smith` to the `friends` database file. Here's what the file looks like when you're finished:

```
Bob Smith   555-1212
Mary Jones  555-5555
Tom Adams   555-7777
John Smith  555-4444
```

Now you can ask the computer to show you Bob Smith's telephone number. Because two lines contain `Smith`, you make it clear in the search expression that you want to see `Bob Smith` and not `John Smith`.

Here's how the search expression looks:

```
awk '/Bob Smith/ {print $1, $2, $3}'friends
```

The search expression includes the space between the first and last names of `Bob Smith`.

Match only the beginning of the line

You can be clever and tell the computer to match characters from the beginning of the line. You accomplish this feat by including a *caret* (^) as the first character in the search expression. Why would you need to do this? Good question. Look at this database file:

```
123786 Bin 123987
123987 Bin 134444
134444 Bin 123986
133333 Bin 123986
```

It doesn't look like much, but perhaps the first column contains part numbers and the second and third columns contain location numbers in a warehouse. Now you want the computer to show you the location of all the parts that have a part number beginning with 123.

At first glance, you may think of just matching the characters, as I just showed you. The command would look like this:

```
awk '/123/ {print $2, $3}'inventory
```

However, this command causes all the rows to be returned by your computer because each row has the pattern 123 in it. What you really want is to match just the first column. Here's what you need to type:

```
awk '/^123/ {print $2, $3}'inventory
```

Now only the first two rows meet the search expression.

Choose the column to match

You can specify the column that contains the data to match as part of the search expression. Say that you want the computer to find all the rows that have the pattern 123 at the beginning of column 3. In addition, you know that the column can have other characters in the column after the pattern 123. Use this expression:

```
awk '$3 ~ /^123*/ {print $1}'inventory
```

The $3 represents the column that you want to have searched.

The tilde character (~) tells the computer that you are looking for a match. It's like an == operator that is used in the if statement.

The caret (^) tells the computer to start matching at the beginning of the column.

The asterisk (*) tells the computer that it is okay if there are other characters in the column in addition to the ones that you are seeking.

Do not match

You can also tell the computer to show rows that don't match the search expression. To display the part numbers that are *not* in locations that begin with 123, use the following expression:

```
awk '$3 !~ /^123*/ {print $1}'inventory
```

The only difference between this and the preceding search expression is the *not* operator (!) that is placed before the tilde (~). This operator tells the computer "not equal to."

Extract information to a file

You can copy all or part of the data in a database file to another file by using the redirection operator (>). This is simple:

```
awk '/^123/ {print $2, $3}'inventory > locations
```

In this expression, the computer is told to copy to the locations file only columns 2 and 3 of rows from the inventory database file where 123 are the first three characters on the line. You can view the locations file using a text editor such as vi, or you can use your word processor.

Delete information from a file

Your computer can also quickly remove information from a database file. Just give it the correct command, and your computer takes out an eraser and wipes away the row. In reality, the computer rewrites the database file, omitting the unwanted row.

Here's how you do it. The friends database file has a row with information about Tom Adams.

```
Bob Smith    555-1212
Mary Jones   555-5555
Tom Adams    555-7777
John Smith   555-4444
```

Perhaps Tom Adams is no longer your friend. To delete that row from the database file, use the following expressions:

```
awk '$2 !~ /^Adams/ {print $1, $2, $3}'friends > newfriends
rm friends
cp newfriends friends
rm newfriends
```

REMEMBER

Displaying information on the screen

You can pick which columns are displayed from the database file by using the print statement and the column number. Your search must include the following criteria:

✔ Each column that you want to have shown on the screen must be preceded by a dollar sign ($).

✔ A comma must separate each column reference.

Here's how the expression looks:

```
awk '/123/ {print $2, $3}'inventory
```

Here's a blow-by-blow account of what's happening:

1. `awk '$2 !~ /^Adams/ {print $1, $2, $3}'friends >` tells your computer to find rows that don't contain the name `Adams` in the second column. When the computer finds a column that fits the search criteria, all the columns are copied to the new database file called `newfriends`.

2. The row that contains `Adams` is not copied to the `newfriends` database file.

3. `rm friends` deletes the `friends` database file.

4. `cp newfriends friends` copies the `newfriends` database file to a new file called `friends`. Now both database files contain the same information.

5. `rm newfriends` deletes the `newfriends` database file, leaving you with the revised `friends` database file.

Test your newfound knowledge

1. What is the difference between a file and a database?

    a. Four letters

    b. A file is something that you use to break out of jail; a database is too large.

    c. A database must store information in an organized format, but a file doesn't.

    d. A file is used to hold data, while a database is what they call home in *Star Trek*.

2. How can some data in a database file be copied to another file?

    a. Use the Model 1470 Xerox color copier.

    b. Use a No. 2 pencil to copy the data from the screen.

    c. No one would ever want to copy data from the database file.

    d. Use the redirection operator.

Chapter 17

Making Your Program Print Stuff Out

*S*howing information on the screen is fine if you're looking for a quick answer to a question. But taking the information away with you is a bit difficult. (You grab the monitor and I'll take the computer.)

You don't have to break your back lugging the computer around with you. Nor do you have to get writer's cramp jotting down the information on scrap paper. A better way is to have your computer send the information to the printer.

Give Me Some]p Service

A printer is similar to your computer screen. It takes characters from your computer and displays them. Instead of displaying information on a monitor, the information is printed on paper.

Many kinds of printers can be connected to your computer. The following are a few examples:

  ✔ Laser printer

  ✔ Dot matrix printer

  ✔ Inkjet printer

You don't have to concern yourself with the kind of printer that is attached to your computer when you write information to your printer. You do have to know how to tell your computer to send the information to the printer. This is done by calling the]p utility. This utility takes the information that you supply and makes sure that it is properly sent to the printer.

Essentially, you worry about the text that you want to have printed, and the lp utility worries about how to get it to the printer. And, of course, the printer worries about how to get the information on the paper.

Printing a Line of Text

The simplest program that you can write is to display a line of text on the screen using the echo command.

Here's how you do this:

```
echo "Hello world."
```

Your screen thus shows:

```
Hello World.
```

You can send the same line of text directly to the printer by using the pipe operator (|) followed by the call to the lp utility.

```
echo "Hello world." | lp
```

Your computer is told to use the echo command to display the phrase Hello world. The computer is then told to take those characters and send them to the lp utility. This is called *piping* (nerds call this taking the output of the echo command and piping it into the input of the lp utility). The lp utility then takes these characters and sends them to your printer.

Printing a File

Sending a line of text directly to the printer isn't very smart programming. A better sign of programming is not to repeat any code.

In this example, the program is calling the lp utility a couple of times:

```
echo "Hello world." | lp
echo "How are you doing?" | lp
```

A better way is to write all the text to a file. When the information is safely stored on your hard disk, you can send the entire file to the lp utility. Here's how you put all of the text into a file called myfile:

Pipes and redirection (and other UNIX 101 things)

Don't be concerned if you're a little confused about pipes, redirection, and all the other nerdy stuff.

You're a traffic cop trying to keep cars (information) flowing in the right direction. You can give one of three signals to control the flow: none, redirection (>), or piping (|).

Consider that you want traffic to flow normally. The best signal to give is none. Nerds call this sending information to *standard out,* which is usually the screen. When the cars get there, they stop. The trip is over.

Now, you want to change flow away from the normal destination (the screen) and send it to another destination (a file). Just give the computer the redirection signal (>). When the cars get there, they also stop. The trip is over.

Finally, you may want to send the traffic to another highway (utility). Give your computer the pipe signal (|). When the cars get there, they don't stop. Instead, another program takes control, and the cars keep moving.

```
echo "Hello world." > myfile
echo "How are you doing?" >> myfile
```

Next, you can use the cat utility to read the information from the file and send it to the lp utility for printing. The cat utility only requires the name of your file. You issue the following command:

```
cat myfile | lp
```

Your computer is told to call the cat utility. The cat utility opens the file myfile and reads each character. Normally, as each character is read, the cat utility displays the character on the screen. The pipe character (|), however, tells the computer to send the characters to the lp utility rather than to the screen. The lp utility then passes the characters to the printer.

Printing a Database

You print information in a database in the same way that you print a file. First, you create a database as follows:

```
echo "Bob Smith 555-1212" >> friends
echo "Mary Jones 555-5555" >> friends
echo "Tom Adams 555-7777" >> friends
```

Each line of this program appends the information to the `friends` database. After the program finishes, the database contains the names and telephone numbers of three persons.

You use the following command to print all of the information from the database:

```
cat friends | lp
```

This is the same way that you print the contents of a file.

Printing the whole database is sometimes useful, but frequently you want to print only a portion of the information. To do this, you need to call the `awk` utility (which is discussed in Chapter 16).

Use the following command to print all of the information in the database that refers to our friend `Smith`.

```
awk '/Smith/ {print $1, $2, $3}'friends | lp
```

This command tells your computer to take the following steps:

1. Look for the character `Smith` in the database file `friends`.
2. Send the first, second, and third column of all rows that match `Smith` to the `lp` utility.
3. Tell the `lp` utility to send the rows received from the `awk` utility to the printer.

Avoid searching again

One major drawback to sending the results of your search directly to the printer is telling the computer to search the database each time that you want to reprint the information. This is time consuming, because your computer must perform the same task repeatedly.

A better way is to tell the computer to put the results of the search into a file and then send the file to the printer. You issue the following commands to do this:

```
awk '/Smith/ {print $1, $2, $3}'friends > myfriends
cat myfriends | lp
```

This is what's happening:

1. The computer is told to use the awk utility to find rows in the friends database that contain the word Smith.

2. Columns 1, 2, and 3 of each of those rows are copied to the myfriends file.

3. The cat utility is called to read the myfriends file into the lp utility.

4. The lp utility then sends the contents of the myfriends file to the printer.

Printing comments before the data

Sometimes you need to print comments (such as the stuff you have for the screen display) before the information from the database is printed. This procedure isn't so difficult:

```
echo "Here are some of my best friends" > myfriends
awk '/Smith/ {print $1, $2, $3}'friends >> myfriends
cat myfriends | lp
```

This is how it works:

1. The first line tells the computer to copy a comment to the file called myfriends.

2. The second line tells the computer to find rows that contain Smith and to append the entire row to the file called myfriends. This means that the data appears below the comments in the file.

3. The last line tells the computer to use the cat utility to send the contents of the file myfriends to the lp utility for printing.

Printing comments after the data

You can also print comments after the data. Issue the following commands to do just this:

```
awk '/Smith/ {print $1, $2, $3}'friends > myfriends
echo "I have more friends than this." >> myfriends
cat myfriends | lp
```

This is the same technique that is used in the preceding example except that the comment statement appears below the call to the awk utility.

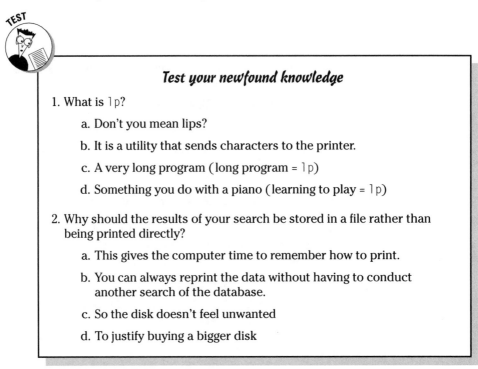

Test your newfound knowledge

1. What is 1p?

    a. Don't you mean lips?

    b. It is a utility that sends characters to the printer.

    c. A very long program (long program = 1p)

    d. Something you do with a piano (learning to play = 1p)

2. Why should the results of your search be stored in a file rather than being printed directly?

    a. This gives the computer time to remember how to print.

    b. You can always reprint the data without having to conduct another search of the database.

    c. So the disk doesn't feel unwanted

    d. To justify buying a bigger disk

Part VII

Debugging Your Program

The 5th Wave · By Rich Tennant

"OOPS - HERE'S THE PROBLEM. SOMETHING'S CAUSING SHORTS IN THE MAINFRAME."

In this part . . .

Chances are that after building your first program, you'll discover that the program doesn't just work the way that you had in mind. Geez. There could be a bug in your program! What next? It's time to *debug* your program. Don't fret. You discover the best ways to debug your programs in this part.

Chapter 18

Stamping Out Bugs in Your Program

. . . .

. . . .

*Y*ou've created your dream UNIX program. It tracks of all those significant others in your life, so you don't have two of them showing up on your doorstep at the same time. Well, what's that saying about mice and men? Your program just missed the mark. It lost track of one. Now you're in hot water.

You have to get yourself out of this trouble. However, there are steps that you can take to correct your program so that the mistake doesn't happen again.

What Is a Bug?

Your program doesn't work because there is a bug in the program. Now don't go looking for your bug spray. That can only damage your computer. Any problem with a program can be called a *bug*. Something has to be blamed for the problem (of course, not the programmer). So why not blame this tiny little critter that scares everyone when it quietly crawls across the floor?

The bug in your program may not be real, but the problem that causes your program to work incorrectly is very real. The following are some common reasons why programs don't work:

✔ An instruction is out of place.

  It's like putting the cart before the horse.

✔ The wrong instruction is given to your computer.

  It's like telling your computer to move on a red light. It's the right time in your program to make a decision, but it's the wrong decision.

- ✓ The wrong word is used.

  Instead of using a word that your computer understands, you use sort of a different word (which looked like the right word to you).

- ✓ You put the word in the wrong place.

  Nerds call this using the wrong *syntax*. It's like saying, "I'm Hawaii to going" when you mean to say, "I'm going to Hawaii."

How a bug gets into your program

Bugs fly in the open window and land on your computer's hard drive just in the spot where your program is stored. (Don't believe it if anyone tells you that story.)

Bugs get into your program in very predictable ways:

- ✓ You rush to write code without first planning what you want to write.

- ✓ Due to typographical errors (whoops)

- ✓ Because of poor computer-language grammar. Grammar checkers don't catch the misuse of words that make up computer languages.

- ✓ You put some code in the wrong place.

- ✓ You guess at the proper word to use. (You didn't want to get up. The book was on the shelf downstairs.)

Don't be too concerned if you find a bug in your program. There are bugs in every program, even those that are written by Bill Gates's people. But just because you have something in common with the pros doesn't mean that you can ignore stamping out the bug.

Don't lose the war

Trying to get your program to work correctly is a test of persistence between you and the bug. This task can become very frustrating, almost to the point where you want to give up.

You should remember the following items when debugging your program:

- ✓ Computers do what they are told to do.

  If the computer is doing something other than what you intended, you are giving it the wrong instruction.

- Don't work around the bug.

  It's like being caught at the office without an umbrella in the middle of a downpour. You can work around the problem by waiting until it stops raining. However, you face the same situation the next time that there's a downpour. The smart solution is to leave an inexpensive umbrella in the office.

- Remember that most bugs are simple and obvious.

  However, your debugging gets more difficult as the complexity of your program increases.

Here is a hidden reward for being persistent about debugging your program: Your knowledge of UNIX programming grows tremendously. After you find the answer to the problem, you most likely never forget it.

Retracing Your Steps

You begin to find why your program isn't working by reviewing each line of your program. This can become a time-consuming task depending on which technique you use.

Here are a few common ways that programmers tackle this job:

- Review each line of code, looking for common problems.
- Watch each line of code as your computer reads the instructions.
- Have the computer check your code for syntax errors.

You must trace your entire program, no matter how insurmountable the review process seems. This is the only way to get your program to run correctly.

Proofread your code

Pretend that you are your computer; then begin reading your program just like the computer would read it. Follow each direction carefully.

This may sound absurd. How can you stuff things into your computer's memory? How can you display characters on the screen? You can't, but you can take a pencil and a piece of paper and draw computer memory and a screen. One sheet of paper can be the memory and another the screen. It's that simple.

Consider that the following program isn't working. It says "Hello" to all of your friends and then "Good-bye" — but keeps repeating these messages endlessly.

```
#!/bin/csh
@ flag = 1
while ($flag == 1)
foreach friend (Bob Mary Sue)
echo "Hello $friend."
end
echo "Good-bye!"
@ flag = 1
end
```

The first thing that you need to do is to indent your code to make it readable:

```
#!/bin/csh
@ flag = 1
while ($flag == 1)
        foreach friend (Bob Mary Sue)
            echo "Hello $friend."
        end
    echo "Good-bye!"
    @ flag = 1
end
```

Next, on the piece of paper that represents your computer's memory, write the line @ flag = 1. That's what your computer is doing.

The next instruction tells your computer to check if the value of $flag is 1. So look at the piece of paper, and you can see that it is equal to 1 (and for this you went to college). This means that you must follow the instructions inside the loop.

The first of these instructions tells the computer to place the string Bob into the string variable friend. Write this on the paper. Your paper version of your computer memory should be like this:

```
@ flag = 1
set friend = "Bob"
```

The next line tells the computer to display Hello Bob. on the screen. Write this greeting on the paper that you are using as your screen.

Continue this process until all of the names are on the screen. Your paper should look like this:

```
Hello Bob.
Hello Mary.
Hello Sue.
```

There aren't any more values in the foreach loop, so the loop ends and the next line is executed. This line tells your computer to display Good-bye! on the screen.

Now write this same line on your paper:

```
Hello Bob.
Hello Mary.
Hello Sue.
Good-bye!
```

The next line tells your computer to place the value 1 in the $flag variable. Go to the piece of paper that contains the variables, find the $flag variable, and erase whatever value is there. Place a 1 next to the $flag variable.

Why erase the value? You're doing exactly what your computer does when it reads your program. It always overwrites whatever value is already assigned to a variable (picky, picky).

Return to the top of the loop, check the value of the $flag variable, and repeat the process.

Wait! Do you see the bug? The computer keeps displaying the same messages because the value of the $flag variable is always 1.

Here's how you fix the bug:

```
#!/bin/csh
@ flag = 1
while ($flag == 1)
        foreach friend (Bob Mary Sue)
          echo "Hello $friend."
        end
   echo "Good-bye!"
  @ flag = 0
end
```

The value of @ flag is changed to 0 at the end of the loop.

Look at your code while the program is running

Reviewing each line of your code is fine for short programs, but it is a nightmare if you're using this method to debug a much larger and more complex program.

Debugging a program (that's talk for finding the problem with your program) is tedious work. Regardless of what method you use to locate the problem, you still need to review the lines of your code as the final step in this process.

Not being able to see your instructions while your program is running is a drawback when debugging your program. You simply can't see what's happening in that black box.

Here are two ways that you can solve this problem. I'll assume here that your program is named `myprogram` and the you are using the C shell.

- ✔ Use the `-v` option, called the *verbose option,* to tell your computer to display each line of code before it executes it. You use the following expression:

```
% csh -v myprogram
```

  The C shell is called explicitly with the `-v` option and the name of your program.

- ✔ Use the `-x` option, called the *echo option,* to have your computer display each line after it executes it. Here's how you do this:

```
% csh -x myprogram
```

The major difference between these two methods is that `-v` shows you the instruction before the computer executes it, and `-x` shows it to you after the instruction is executed.

Let the computer check your work

Here's a useful method to let your computer make sure that you use the correct words of the computer language. (I'm again using the C shell.)

```
% csh -n myprogram
```

This is called the *syntax checking* option. The computer doesn't execute any instructions in the program. Instead, it looks for reserved words and lets you know if any of them are missing or in error.

The syntax checking option does not check the following items:

- ✔ Putting the instruction in the wrong place in your program
- ✔ Placing the wrong value in a variable
- ✔ Giving the computer the wrong instruction

You can consider the syntax checking option as a grammar checker for the C shell language.

Laying a Trap for the Bug

Sometimes you can look at your code until you can't see straight and you still can't determine why your program isn't working. This can become very frustrating, but don't give up. Instead, try another tactic.

Here are some good fallback plans that you can try:

- ✔ Set flags for yourself throughout the program.

  A *flag* is a message that is displayed on the screen to tell you what part of your program is currently being read by your computer.

- ✔ Display the value of all the variables in your program on the screen.

  This gives you a glimpse of what's happening behind the scenes.

- ✔ Turn parts of your program off and on.

  This helps you to isolate the part of your program that is causing the trouble.

Just use a little common sense when using any of these methods. You have to decide where to place the flags and which parts of your program you turn off and on.

Setting flags

A *flag* is simply a message that is displayed on the screen. The message can be as simple as "I made it this far."

Here's how you use flags:

```
#!/bin/csh
@ flag = 1
echo "Outside of while loop"
while ($flag == 1)
   echo "inside of while loop"
       foreach friend (Bob Mary Sue)
             echo "inside of foreach loop"
             echo "Hello $friend."
       end
   echo "outside of foreach loop"
   echo "Good-bye!"
   @ flag = 1
   echo "last line in while loop"
end
echo "last line in the program"
```

This is what you see on the screen when you run this program:

```
Outside of while loop
inside of while loop
inside of foreach loop
Hello Bob.
inside of foreach loop
Hello Mary.
inside of foreach loop
Hello Sue.
outside of foreach loop
Good-bye!
last line in while loop
inside of while loop
inside of foreach loop
Hello Bob.
inside of foreach loop
Hello Mary.
inside of foreach loop
Hello Sue.
outside of foreach loop
Good-bye!
last line in while loop
```

Take a close look at these flags. Do you see anything strange? Here are some clues:

- ✔ All of the flags inside the `while` loop are repeated. They are repeated endlessly if you run this program.
- ✔ The flag `last line in the program` doesn't appear on the screen.

Where is the problem? The computer enters the `while` loop but doesn't leave the `while` loop.

Display hidden values

You can ask the computer to show you values of variables while the program is running. This method can be combined with the flag method to give you more clues to the puzzle.

Here's how you use this method:

```
#!/bin/csh
@ flag = 1
echo "Outside of while loop flag = $flag"
while ($flag == 1)
   echo "inside of while loop flag = $flag "
        foreach friend (Bob Mary Sue)
             echo "inside of foreach loop flag = $flag "
             echo "Hello $friend."
        end
   echo "outside of foreach loop flag = $flag "
   echo "Good-bye!"
   @ flag = 1
   echo "last line in while loop flag = $flag "
end
echo "last line in the program flag = $flag "
```

Here's what you see on the screen as a result:

```
Outside of while loop flag = 1
inside of while loop flag = 1
inside of foreach loop flag = 1
Hello Bob.
inside of foreach loop flag = 1
```

(continued)

(continued)

```
Hello Mary.
inside of foreach loop flag = 1
Hello Sue.
outside of foreach loop flag = 1
Good-bye!
last line in while loop flag = 1
inside of while loop flag = 1
inside of foreach loop flag = 1
Hello Bob.
inside of foreach loop flag = 1
Hello Mary.
inside of foreach loop flag = 1
Hello Sue.
outside of foreach loop flag = 1
Good-bye!
last line in while loop flag = 1
```

Now you realize that the @ flag variable in your program is never assigned the value of 0. You know the cause of the problem.

Using a file to help find the problem

Displaying flags and the value of variables on the screen is helpful. However, with some programs this isn't practical. There is just too much information to keep on the screen.

A better approach is to have the computer save the stuff that appears on the screen to a file. Here's how you do this:

```
myprogram > flagfile
```

In this example, the computer is told to run myprogram and to redirect to the file flagfile anything that goes to the screen. You can review the flagfile using a text editor such as vi.

Here's how you use vi to review a file:

```
vi flagfile
```

If you really want to get down and dirty trying to locate the trouble inside your program, you can print a copy of the file. This can be used as a guide when you review lines in your program.

Here's how you print a copy of the file:

```
cat flagfile | lp
```

Turning off parts of your program

Another beneficial method that programmers use to find trouble spots in their program is to turn parts of the program off and on.

The first step is to place the comment character (#) as the first character of each line of the program:

```
#!/bin/csh
#@ flag = 1
#while ($flag == 1)
#      foreach friend (Bob Mary Sue)
#           echo "inside of foreach loop flag = $flag "
#           echo "Hello $friend."
#      end
#   echo "Good-bye!"
#   @ flag = 1
#end
```

Lines that begin with a comment character are ignored by the computer, except where the first line of the program only contains the comment character. This line tells the computer to start the C shell.

Next, remove the comment character from lines that are required to perform the same task. For example, the foreach loop and the lines within the foreach loop display a greeting to your friend. This is one task.

Here's what the program looks like:

```
#!/bin/csh
#@ flag = 1
#while ($flag == 1)
      foreach friend (Bob Mary Sue)
           echo "inside of foreach loop flag = $flag "
           echo "Hello $friend."
      end
#   echo "Good-bye!"
#   @ flag = 1
#end
```

The computer starts the C shell. The next two lines are ignored because they are comments. The foreach loop and the code inside this loop are executed, and the program ends.

This process tells you that the problem is not with the foreach loop. It must be somewhere else.

Move to the next line, which displays a farewell message, and remove the comment character. Here's how it should look:

```
#!/bin/csh
#@ flag = 1
#while ($flag == 1)
        foreach friend (Bob Mary Sue)
            echo "inside of foreach loop flag = $flag "
            echo "Hello $friend."
        end
    echo "Good-bye!"
#  @ flag = 1
#end
```

You then see that the program works fine.

The only part of the program that isn't turned on is the while loop and related instructions. By the process of elimination, you know that the problem with the program is in the while loop.

You can be sure of this fact by removing the rest of the comments from the program; then run the program again. Here's what it looks like:

```
#!/bin/csh
@ flag = 1
while ($flag == 1)
        foreach friend (Bob Mary Sue)
            echo "inside of foreach loop flag = $flag "
            echo "Hello $friend."
        end
    echo "Good-bye!"
  @ flag = 1
end
```

You're correct. Now the program no longer works, and you can concentrate your troubleshooting on the while loop.

Running parts of your program by hand

Many UNIX programs are built from subprograms. Some of these are C shell scripts that you or your friends build. Others are UNIX utilities that have been around for years. All subprograms can be run from the command prompt as well as from inside your program.

Instead of running your large program many times to find the problem, you can run each subprogram from outside your program to see if the subprogram is causing the problem.

This technique is especially useful when your program uses the awk utility. This utility searches a database file for a particular pattern of characters (refer to Chapter 16).

A common place for trouble to occur is with the expression that is used in the awk utility. You simply don't ask the awk utility the right question; therefore, it comes up with the wrong answer.

You can modify the expression and execute the awk utility from the command line rather than from within your program. This strategy speeds the debugging process.

Here's how you do this:

```
awk '/123/ {print $2, $3}'inventory
```

This command executes the awk utility on the command line and asks it to display the second and third columns from the inventory file for each row that contains the characters 123.

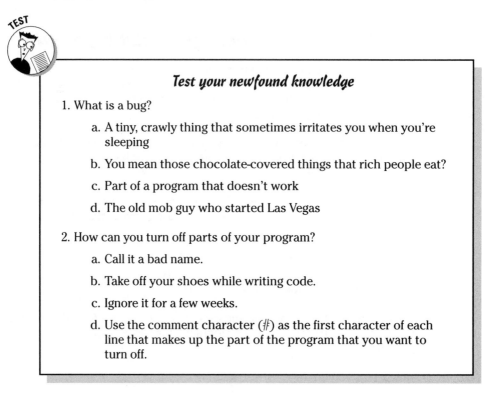

Test your newfound knowledge

1. What is a bug?

    a. A tiny, crawly thing that sometimes irritates you when you're sleeping

    b. You mean those chocolate-covered things that rich people eat?

    c. Part of a program that doesn't work

    d. The old mob guy who started Las Vegas

2. How can you turn off parts of your program?

    a. Call it a bad name.

    b. Take off your shoes while writing code.

    c. Ignore it for a few weeks.

    d. Use the comment character (#) as the first character of each line that makes up the part of the program that you want to turn off.

Part VIII
The Part of Tens

The 5th Wave

By Rich Tennant

©RICHTENNANT

"YEAH, I USED TO WORK ON REFRIGERATORS, WASHING MACHINES, STUFF LIKE THAT—HOW'D YOU GUESS?"

In this part . . .

In this part, I get to tell you all sort of things that just didn't come up in the regular chapters or things that were too involved to get into. Here you can find out about the most useful UNIX utilities (and I know you've been waiting for the chance). You can also stumble across sources for more UNIX programming information. And to top everything off, you even get in this part a *potpourri* of topics that I couldn't fit elsewhere.

Chapter 19

The Ten Most Useful UNIX Utilities

*O*ne of the biggest chores involved in building a UNIX program is assembling a bunch of utility programs that you or someone else has written. Each of these utility programs specializes in doing something well. This is the whole philosophy of UNIX — creating small utility programs, each performing one task very well.

Hundreds of utility programs are distributed with the UNIX operating system, and they're all available on the Internet. This book isn't big enough to discuss all the utilities, but I want to show you my top ten list. (My list may vary from David Letterman's list, of course.)

I present only the basic information for using each utility — just enough to whet your appetite. You can use the man pages in the online documentation (available on most UNIX computers) to find out the details of how to use each of these utility programs.

For example, to learn everything you can about the troff utility (discussed in the next section), type the following command:

```
man troff
```

When you press the Enter key, UNIX displays the manual pages that discuss the `troff` utility in detail.

You enter on the command line (at the UNIX prompt) all the commands that I mention in this chapter. Thus, if you are using the C shell, your command would look like this:

```
% man troff
```

Printing Fancy Stuff: troff

Most of the printing you do in UNIX is the plain-Jane type. Whichever font and type size are available on your printer are the ones used for your document. Whatever happened to all the fancy stuff that you've seen in Windows and Mac programs, such as designing a page layout and using fancy type?

Nothing. If you have a printer that offers these features, UNIX can send instructions to your printer to make your documents look fancy. The trick is to use the `troff` utility. It interprets special codes into commands that tell the printer to turn on those fancy features.

If you want "Hello, world." to appear in 12-point type in your document, for example, you type the following line in your document file. A document file is a file on your computer's disk that contains the text that you want printed in your document. This file can be created using a text editor such as `vi` or from one of your own programs.

```
.ps 12
Hello, world.
```

The `.ps 12` special code tells the `troff` utility that from this point on you want to use 12-point type in your document. The `troff` utility then sends to the printer a printer code for 12-point type. If you want to change to another point size, then you'll need to enter a different code into your document.

Now use the `troff` utility to send a `greeting` to the printer:

```
troff greeting
```

And then change the font to roman:

```
.ps 12
.ft roman
Hello, world.
```

This example tells the troff utility that you want to use 12-point type (.ps 12) in the roman font (.ft roman). These settings remain in effect until you change the values of these codes in your document.

Keep in mind that using these codes in your documents involves one major drawback: Only the troff utility reads them. Don't forget that the lp utility, too, is used to print your document (refer to Chapter 17). However, the lp utility prints all the characters that you enter into the document. The lp utility does not recognize, for example, that .ps12 is a special code that shouldn't be printed because the code is used to give the troff utility an instruction.

Checking Your Spelling: spell

Few people can pose even a minor threat to the national spelling bee champion's crown, and the typical error-filled business document proves my point. A misspelling is where the writer doesn't know the correct spelling of the word. In comparison, a typo is where the writer knows the correct spelling of the word but inadvertently presses the wrong key on the keyboard when typing the word in the document. Most people can come up with a host of excuses:

- ✔ "My secretary is a poor proofreader." (Do you even have a secretary?)

- ✔ "I was in a rush and didn't catch that mistake." (You read the document ten times.)

- ✔ "He'll never notice that it's misspelled." (Oh, how you wish that this one were true!)

- ✔ "She'll know what I mean." (She'll also know that you don't know how to spell.)

Now you have no excuse for misspellings or typos in the documents you create in UNIX unless you are too lazy to let spell check the spelling for you. This simple spell-checker utility reads your documents and then displays the words it cannot find in its dictionary file.

Suppose that you type the following text in a document and then save the document in a file called letter:

```
Dear Mary,

We hab a goo time Saturday. Let's do it again soon.
```

Use the following command to have spell take a look at the file:

```
spell letter
```

The following lines are then displayed on-screen:

```
hab
goo
```

Using the `spell` utility has a few drawbacks, however:

- ✔ `spell` catches any word it didn't find in its dictionary file, but the word may not necessarily be misspelled. The `spell` utility really compares the words in your document against those that the programmer entered into the `spell` utility's dictionary. For example, in an address where the town is Ridgefield Park, the `spell` utility reports that Ridgefield is incorrectly spelled. In fact, Ridgefield is correct but just doesn't appear in the `spell` utility's dictionary.

- ✔ `spell` lists misspelled words — but because it doesn't show you where they are in the document, you have to find them yourself.

Sorting Stuff in Your Files: `sort`

Your programs can produce a list of names, but someone who uses your program may want the list sorted. You can spend many evenings researching ways to write a program to sort the list, or you can simply use the `sort` utility.

Suppose that you have listed some names in a file called `names`. You can type the following line to sort the list:

```
sort names
```

The `sort` utility rearranges a list in ascending order (where the As come before the Bs and the 1s come before the 2s) and places a lowercase letter in front of its equivalent uppercase letter. You can change to descending order (where the Bs come before the As and the 2s come before the 1s) by using the `-r` option:

```
sort -r names
```

To have the `sort` utility ignore the case distinction, use the `-f` option:

```
sort -f names
```

Another sort option tells the `sort` utility to order the file in numerical order (`-n`). Still another sort option tells the sort utility to order by month (`-m`). The `m` sort option places January before February, February before March, and so on.

One drawback when you are using the sort utility is that the new sorted list is not saved in the same file that contains the original, unsorted list. When you re-sort the names file, the results are displayed on-screen unless you use the redirection operator (>) to save the information in another file. (For a description of redirection operators, refer to the sidebar "The inside story of redirection" in Chapter 5.)

What if you want the ordered information to be placed in the same file? Here's how you do it:

```
sort -f names > newnames
mv newnames > names
```

The sort utility reorders the names file (ignoring the case distinction) and saves the sorted information in the newnames file. The last line renames the newnames file to the old file called names by using the move (mv) command.

Checking Differences between Files: diff

When you begin programming in UNIX, you inevitably come across the problem of having two files with practically the same name that contain your program. How do you find the differences between the files?

You can compare each file line by line yourself, or you can let the diff utility do it for you. When you type the following line on the command line, you tell the diff utility to read file1 and file2 and to tell you the lines that are different in each file:

```
diff file1 file2
```

Let's say you executed the diff utility from the command line. Here's what the diff utility might report back to you on the screen:

```
<programming is fun.
>I hate computers.
```

Lines that begin with the less-than sign (<) are lines that diff found only in file1; lines that begin with the greater-than sign (>) are lines diff found only in file2. Lines in either file that aren't displayed by the diff utility are lines found in both files. (For more information about the < and > redirection operators, refer to the sidebar "The inside story of redirection" in Chapter 5.)

Changing Characters in a Large File: sed

If you try to modify an extremely large file, you may experience a serious problem: Your computer can run out of memory (called a *buffer*) to store the file. This means that there is no more room inside your computer to store the text contained in the file.

Some text editors load a file into a buffer before you can begin editing the text in the file. If a file is too large for the buffer, you can't use the editor to change the text. This limitation isn't a problem for the sed utility, however: This text editor doesn't try to load the entire file into memory — it just reads one line at a time from your file; makes changes to the line; and sends it back to the file on your hard disk.

Suppose that you want to remove all lines in the names file that contain the word *Bob*. (I wonder what Bob did to deserve that treatment.) sed normally displays the changed text on the screen. This doesn't help us because we want the changed information to be stored in the same file. So use the redirection operator (>) to have the output of sed redirected to a file called names.tmp. After the changes are safely in this file, use the mv command to change the name of the names.tmp file to the names file. Now you have replaced the old names file with the changed version of the file. Here's what you need to do:

```
sed '/Bob/d' names > names.tmp
mv names.tmp names
```

The target of your search is any character you place between the slash marks (/). The d is the sed command for deleting a line.

Rather than delete lines that have the word *Bob* in them, replace Bob with Mike:

```
sed 's/Bob/Mike/' names > names.tmp
mv names.tmp names
```

The s is the sed command for substituting characters. The characters you type between the first two slash marks are replaced with the characters you type between the second and third slash marks.

Now remove just the word Mike:

```
sed 's/Mike//' names > names.tmp
mv names.tmp names
```

This line is similar to the preceding example, except that you don't type a value between the second and third slash marks. The reason is that you're telling the sed utility to substitute "nothing" for the name Mike.

Breaking a Large File: split

Because a large file can be troublesome to work with in UNIX, why not break down the file into a bunch of other files?

You can manually break down a file by copying and deleting the text in the file, but this process can become cumbersome. A better method is to make the split utility do the job for you. By default, split automatically divides your file into 1,000-line files. The new files are named xaa, xab, and so on.

Suppose that you have a file named phonebook that has 2,500 entries in it. (Boy, do you have a truckload of friends!) To break this file into several files, you type the following line:

```
split phonebook
```

The split utility then creates three files. The first two files have 1,000 entries apiece. The third file holds 500 entries (the entries that remain). This list shows the filenames created by the split utility:

```
xaa
xab
xac
```

You can specify the maximum number of lines that are to be in each file by using the -n option.

```
split -n <filename>
```

Substitute the number of lines you want for n. In this next example, I use the split utility to divide the phonebook file into smaller files. Each of these smaller files should have no more than 100 lines. (And if each line represents one entry in the telephone book, I am telling the split utility to split the phonebook into files of 100 entries each.)

```
split -100 phonebook
```

Finding Information in a File: grep

What can you do if you want to know which file in the current directory has the name Bob in it? You can use commands in a text editor to help find Bob — or you can use the grep utility. In the case of a text editor, you must first run the text editor and load the file before you can begin searching for Bob. However, with the `grep` utility, you specify the word that you want to search for when you execute this utility. The `grep` utility searches a file for a set of characters and displays all the lines that contain those characters.

If you want to find all the lines that have `Bob` in the `namefile`, for example, you type this line:

```
grep Bob namefile
```

Now suppose that you want to find in your files the name of a specific Bob: Bob Smith. If your search criterion contains a space, you have to place quotation marks around the entire phrase:

```
grep "Bob Smith" namefile
```

Sometimes you don't know which file contains the name `Bob`. You know that it's one of the hundreds of files in the current directory, but you don't know which one. (That's what I call organization!) Type the following line:

```
grep Bob *
```

The asterisk (*) replaces the name of the file to be searched. The asterisk, which is a wildcard, tells the `grep` utility to search all the files in the current directory. A wildcard is a symbol that tells UNIX to use any file name that it finds on the hard disk.

Sending Files Electronically: `ftp`

You can ship your files electronically to any Internet location in the world by using the `ftp` utility. This utility enables you to link your computer to a remote computer and then send or receive one or more files. To begin, type this line:

```
ftp othercomputer
```

In this example, the `ftp` utility tries to connect your computer to the computer named `othercomputer`. If the `ftp` utility is successful, you're prompted to enter your password.

If you don't get kicked out of the `othercomputer` (meaning that you could log onto the computer because your login ID and password were accepted by the `othercomputer`), you see the `ftp` command prompt, which looks like this:

```
ftp>
```

You can then enter `ftp` commands that instruct the `ftp` utility to perform a task.

Now suppose that you want to transfer the `datebook` file that is stored on the `othercomputer` to your computer. Just type this line:

```
ftp> get datebook
```

The `ftp` utility handles the file transfer for you. What happens, however, if you want to ship the same file to the other computer? The `ftp` utility is willing to help:

```
ftp> put datebook
```

As long as the `datebook` file is in the current directory, the `ftp` utility does the rest of the work for you, by copying the file to the other computer. The original copy remains on your computer.

When you finish transferring files, you give the `ftp` utility the instruction to say good-bye to the other computer:

```
ftp> bye
```

The `ftp` utility then closes the transmission channel with the other computer and returns the UNIX prompt to your screen.

Don't forget that you can find out more about the `ftp` utility (or any other utility, for that matter), by using the `man` utility that I explain at the beginning of the chapter.

Comparing Files: cmp

At some point, you'll have a need to determine if two files are the same. The best way to answer that question is by letting the `cmp` utility compare the files. The `cmp` utility is similar to the `diff` utility except that the `cmp` utility displays which *character* on a line is different in the files. The `diff` utility simply shows you the *lines* that are different.

The `cmp` utility matches both files line by line and issues a report that specifies where any differences occur. If you have two files that seem to refer to the same program, such as `firstprogram` and `programone`, you can type the following line to compare the files:

```
cmp firstprogram programone
```

The result might look something like this:

```
firstprogram programone differ: char 34, line 3
```

This line indicates that character 34 on line 3 of `programone` is different from character 34 on line 3 in `firstprogram`.

Removing Fields from a Database: cut

A database file is similar to a regular file except that the information is organized into columns and rows. (A column is also called a *field*, and a row is called a *record*.) You can remove fields from a database file by using the `cut` utility. (For more information about databases, refer to Chapter 16.)

Suppose that you have a database file called `phonelist` that contains the following information:

```
Bob Smith    555-1212
Mary Jones   555-5555
Tom Adams    555-7777
```

To remove the names to a file called `names`, you type this line:

```
cut -f1,2 phonelist > names
```

The `-f` option tells the `cut` utility that you want to cut columns 1 and 2 from the `phonelist` file. The redirection operator (`>`) takes the columns that are cut from the `phonelist` file and places them in the `names` file. (To find out about the redirection operators, refer to the sidebar "The inside story of redirection" in Chapter 5.)

Chapter 20

Ten Sources of More UNIX Programming Information

*B*ecause you're a beginner in the area of UNIX programming, there's much more for you to discover. Even professional programmers have to hit the books, take courses, and go to conferences to keep up with the latest changes in technology — and you can expect to do the same. This chapter presents a few suggestions for ways you can find out more about UNIX programming.

Go Back to School at Your Local College

One of the better places to pick up some tricks and tips of the UNIX trade is close to home, at your local college.

You don't have to go to MIT to find out about UNIX programming, and you certainly don't have to be a computer nerd. As I have mentioned frequently in this book, anyone with a little common sense and a great deal of patience can learn to program a computer.

Sometimes you need more help in locating this type of information than a book can provide. You need someone to look over your shoulder until you get on the right track — and that person (the instructor) is usually at your local college.

Many four-year universities and community colleges offer courses in UNIX programming. Give your local college a call to find out when the next course is being offered. Then be sure to find out how to register for the course.

You don't have to go for the whole college degree. These institutions love to have students who just want to brush up on their skills by auditing a course or two. (They hope that you will get hooked and come back for more.)

Attend a Conference

A good source for the latest information about UNIX and UNIX programming is computer conferences. Computer professionals, vendors, and nerd wanna-bes gather at these meetings to exchange ideas. UNIX is such a hot topic these days that UNIX and UNIX programming are discussed at conferences that don't even have UNIX in their name.

Two popular conferences are UNIX Expo and PC Expo, which are widely advertised in trade publications such as *PC Week* and *InfoWorld*. Keep your eyes peeled for these ads, which usually list scheduled speakers and topics. Some presentations cover topics that might be of interest to you (and others may be way over your head!).

Plan to pay for this experience. Conferences are usually held in major cities (and in Hawaii). You have to pay for airfare and accommodations and a fee to get into the conference. You may also have to pay for each presentation you attend.

Join CompuServe

What if you just want to talk with someone who is also beginning to program in UNIX and you can't find anyone around? Just join CompuServe and get connected.

CompuServe offers many discussion groups that focus on computer programming and UNIX programming specifically. After you log in, jump around and find a discussion group related to the topic that interests you. New groups pop up all the time.

Here's how to contact CompuServe:

CompuServe
P.O. Box 20212
5000 Arlington Centre Blvd.
Columbus, OH 43220
800-848-8990

After you sign up and find an interesting area, read through the transcripts of electronic conversations that have already taken place. A wealth of information is at your fingertips. You may want to print some of the more worthwhile discussions for your notebook.

Don't be afraid to join in the conversation — that's the whole point of connecting to a discussion group. Ask questions. As your elementary-school math teacher undoubtedly told you, no question is too stupid to ask. Most people who are tuned in to a discussion group are more than willing to help you. It probably wasn't too long ago that they were UNIX programming novices.

Find a Newsgroup on the Internet

Usenet news is the part of the Internet you can tap into for sources of information from around the world. Each of the newsgroups that comprise this service focus on a particular topic. (If you're still unsure of this Internet stuff, consider books such as *The Internet For Dummies* by John Levine and Carol Baroudi, available from IDG Books Worldwide, Inc.)

Thousands of newsgroups are available. You can use your Internet browser to skim through the available newsgroups and then choose the ones you want to subscribe to (for free!).

Every time you visit Usenet news, your browser displays your list of newsgroups. After you choose one in which you want to participate, your browser shows you all the postings for that group.

To find newsgroups, use keywords with your browser's built-in search feature to quickly skim the list for newsgroups in which you're interested. If you enter the keyword UNIX, for example, a large list of newsgroups that contain information about UNIX appears on-screen.

After you enter a newsgroup, a list of subjects is displayed that briefly describes the related messages people have posted. (The messages can contain anything from meaningful information to just plain garbage.) Skim the subject list to see whether any of them seem interesting. When you find one, open the message and see what that person had to say.

You can post (send) your own message to a newsgroup by using your Internet browser. You can comment on other messages, post questions, or answer questions that other people have posted.

It may take a while until your newsgroup messages get posted. Be patient. Keep watching the subject listings for the newsgroup to see whether anyone responds to your posting.

A word of caution: Just because something gets posted doesn't necessarily mean that it's true. Even someone with good intentions can post incorrect information.

Review Online Documentation

When you have questions about UNIX programming or any of the UNIX utilities, you want your questions answered quickly and accurately. Where can you find a response, though, especially when you're sitting in front of your computer at 2 a.m.?

Ask your computer! One of the best features of UNIX is its man utility, which displays the *man*ual pages for the operating system. If you're puzzled about how to use the sort utility, for example, just type the following at the UNIX command prompt:

```
man sort
```

Your computer then displays the manual for the sort utility. Although the manual isn't as well written as this book, it does provide a complete discussion of topics, including how to implement all the options. What more can you ask for (except for someone else to do the programming!)?

Read Other Books about UNIX

You should expand your knowledge of UNIX in two directions: programming and the operating system. This book covers the programming aspect of your UNIX education. To find out more about the UNIX operating system (the software that, like DOS, runs many computers), pick up a copy of *UNIX For Dummies,* 2nd Edition, and *MORE UNIX For Dummies,* both written by John R. Levine and Margy Levine Young and published by IDG Books Worldwide, Inc.

Subscribe to Computing Magazines

Hit the newsstands and search the racks for computer magazines. A vast array of magazines is available about every imaginable aspect of computing.

Don't limit yourself to newsstands — bookstores and major computer stores also offer a wide selection of computer magazines. Keep your eyes peeled for articles and columns about UNIX and UNIX programming. Those magazines are the ones you should subscribe to.

Also check out trade magazines, such as *UNIX World, PC Week,* and *InfoWorld.* They talk about the latest developments in the computer industry and the world of technology and are a must-read for serious programmers.

Join or Create a UNIX Programming Club

You're probably not the only person in your town or city who's interested in computer programming. Computer clubs are a common gathering place for like-minded folks.

Computer clubs are great places to exchange ideas about all sorts of aspects of computers, including UNIX programming.

Ask around to find your local computer club. Start with the computer teachers in your local school district and the manager of your local computer store. They should have a good idea about whether a club exists. If you can't find a local club, ask the manager of your local computer store to help you organize one.

Ask for Technical Help at Your Local College Computer Lab

If you end up in a bind, stop by the computer lab at your local college or university. All sorts of nerds hang out there who are usually more than happy to give you an opinion about how to solve your problem.

Try to build a friendship with a few of these folks. Before long, you'll become part of the family.

Computer labs are usually open to members of the general student body. The labs are overseen by teaching assistants or advanced computer science majors who are looking to make a few extra dollars. It also helps to take a course or two to become an official student.

Send E-Mail to Authors of Articles about UNIX Programming

One way to quiz the experts is to send an e-mail message to them. Most authors of computer articles and books now include their e-mail address as part of their byline. If you have a question about an article or book topic, ask your question in an e-mail message.

Authors are usually pleased to hear from their readers and do their best to answer questions. Keep in mind, however, that they don't want to become your tutor or your pen pal. Because authors might also be busy with other projects, your request can be a low priority.

Chapter 21

Ten UNIX Programming Topics That Didn't Fit Anywhere Else

- -

In This Chapter

▶ Running programs in the background

▶ Pulling the plug on your program in an emergency

▶ Making shell variables available to subprograms

▶ Preventing other people from altering your code

▶ Translating your files so that you can transfer them between DOS and UNIX

▶ Searching for lost files

▶ Creating a place for programs on your hard disk

▶ Changing characters in a file

▶ Saving your code in an archive file

▶ Stopping your program temporarily

- -

*N*ow that you are at the end of this book (even if you haven't read it yet and just skipped back here to see the possibilities), you probably are wondering whether the information in this book includes everything you need to know about UNIX and UNIX programming.

No, this is just the beginning. This chapter has some tidbits that you may find useful and interesting as you continue your quest to build that killer UNIX program (the one that will make you more money than Bill Gates has).

Creating Programs That Run in the Background

You can make your UNIX program one of those sneaky, stealth applications that quietly goes about doing its thing inside the computer while other programs are running. This type of program, called a *daemon,* lives inside your computer somewhere and can do mischievous things. (Not really — you wouldn't think of writing a program that would destroy your own computer.)

A daemon program is frequently used to process information that doesn't require the use of the keyboard or the screen. An example is a payroll program that crunches numbers in a database and then prints checks. No one has to do anything other than start the program as a daemon:

```
payroll &
```

You insert an ampersand (&) after the name of the program to tell your computer to run the program in the background. In other words, you run it as a daemon (you little devil).

One problem with a daemon is that it stops running when you log off the computer. You can keep it running after you're long gone by using the nohup command followed by the name of the program:

```
nohup payroll
```

Stopping Your Program in an Emergency

You must be prepared to jump into action if your program goes wild. Every programmer experiences this situation while building a new program. During a test, the program keeps running and running (and sort of resembles the Energizer bunny).

This situation can be caused by a number of reasons, such as an endless loop. Before you can find out what went wrong, however, you have to stop the program. If this situation happens on a computer running DOS, you can turn off the computer.

Don't turn off a computer that's running UNIX. Other things may be happening in the background that can't be interrupted (otherwise your system file can be out of sync and must be reset — usually by a system administrator — before you can use your computer again). Instead, you tell the computer to stop your program by using the kill command.

When you use the kill command, you must also identify the program you want to stop. *You* know what you named the program, but you have to find out how your computer identifies it.

You do this by running the `jobs` command . . .

```
jobs
```

. . . which displays all your active programs:

```
[1] + Running payroll
[2] + Running vi
```

The `jobs` command shows you the status of your programs. In this example, two of your programs are running: `payroll` and `vi`. The numbers at the beginning of each line are used to identify each program. To stop a program from running, you use the appropriate number with the `kill` command:

```
kill %1
```

This example tells the computer to kill program 1. (Notice the percent sign followed by the job number.) After your order is carried out, the `kill` command reports back to you that it stopped the program so that you can begin to investigate the cause of the problem.

```
[1] + Terminated payroll
```

Sharing Shell Variables

Whenever you call a subprogram from your program, one common problem is that a variable you create in your program is not available to the subprogram. For example, if your program creates this string variable:

```
set name = "Bob Smith"
```

and you call the subprogram named `payroll` from your program:

```
set name = "Bob Smith"
payroll
```

The `payroll` program doesn't know that the variable `name` exists. The reason is that your computer started another shell called a *subshell*.

Here's how the shell works. (No, it's not under the middle one). When you log on to your computer, your computer starts a shell. A *shell* is the program that translates your wishes to your computer. For more information about shells, refer to Chapter 3.

Your computer creates another copy of the shell for each program you run. Guess what happens when your program runs a subprogram: Another shell is started. When your program or subprogram finishes running, its shell closes.

Variables created in each shell are *local,* which means that only that shell can use the variables (for more information about local variables, refer to the section "Using variables" in Chapter 4). You can make shell variables available to other shells, however, by changing the variable to an environment variable:

```
setenv name = "Bob Smith"
payroll
```

In this example, the payroll program has access to the name variable. Either the program or the subprogram can change the value of name. The change, however, does affect the other copy of the name variable. For example, both the program and the payroll program have access to the name variable with the value Bob Smith because the program makes the name variable an environment variable.

The payroll program can assign Joan Jones to the name variable that affects the name variable in the program. That is, the value of the name variable in the program is changed to Joan Jones.

The next time your subprogram isn't working properly, double check to see whether it is using a variable it cannot access.

Keeping Other People's Hands off Your Code

A major weakness in a UNIX shell program is that your code is available to prying eyes and that some folks just like to change other people's code. This means that anyone who has a copy of your UNIX shell program can look at your code by using vi or any text editor. This is because your UNIX shell program is text — instructions written in English — and is translated by UNIX into machine language as each instruction in your program is followed by your program.

This problem doesn't exist in most programs that are written in other programming languages because the program starts out as text just like your UNIX shell program. However, the program is translated into machine language by a program called a *compiler,* which is stored in a file that is given to anyone who wants to run the program. Therefore, there isn't a copy of the code that anyone other than real nerds can see.

Although you cannot make your shell program into machine language, you can have UNIX prevent unauthorized persons from seeing the code of your program by using the chmod command. The chmod command is used to give everyone else permission to execute your program only. They won't be able to read nor write to your program file. Here's how this is done:

```
chmod o+x payroll
```

This line tells UNIX that anyone can execute your payroll program, but they can't look at your program file and they can't write to your program file. (Refer to Chapter 1 for a few more details — along with alternative commands — for the chmod utility.)

If you really want to lay down the law, you can also limit access of your small group of friends:

```
chmod g+x payroll
```

Only a member of your group can execute your program. (The person in charge of your computer, called the *system administrator,* determines who is in your group.)

Copying Files between DOS and UNIX

Your UNIX program may need to use a bunch of information that is on your personal computer running DOS. For example, say that you have a list of your friends that you saved in a text file format on your PC. A text file is a file that you created using an editor or a word processor that does not have any special formatting characters in the file. The file just has text. (And that's where they got the name.)

Now, the problem is that you want to save the file to a floppy disk, and then copy the file onto your computer that is running UNIX. This process sounds simple, and you've done it thousands of times from one DOS PC to another. But if you try simply copying the file to UNIX, it won't work! I don't go into the details here, but trust me: It just won't work because the formats are not compatible.

But if you're using XENIX, which is a version of UNIX, you can easily overcome this problem: Just use the doscp command to handle all the necessary translations (and indicate a source drive, like I did here with drive A):

```
doscp a:dosdata unixdata
```

This line tells your computer to copy to UNIX the `dosdata` file that's in DOS format on your floppy disk. During the copying process, your computer performs the translation and renames the file in UNIX to `unixdata`.

The following line shows you how to copy a file from UNIX to your DOS floppy disk (again indicating a drive, and in this case I've indicated the A drive):

```
doscp unixdata a:dosdata
```

Your computer copies the `unixdata` file to the DOS floppy disk and, in the process, translates and renames the file.

Finding Lost Files

After you reach your stride in creating UNIX programs, you eventually end up knee-deep in files. They're all over your hard disk: Some you can find immediately, but others are buried in subdirectories.

Finding the file you want can be a huge chore, but you can simplify this task by using the `find` command to do all the work for you. Suppose that you want to find the `payroll` program (the one you haven't touched in more than a year). As long as you can remember the name of the program, you can use the `find` command to search your hard disk:

```
find ~ -name "payroll" -print
```

The tilde (~) tells the computer to begin the search in your home directory. The `find` command begins looking in that directory and continues through all the subdirectories in your home directory. The `-name` option tells the computer that the next word is the name of the program, which is `payroll`. Finally, the `-print` option tells the computer to display the location on your screen.

Creating Your Own Place on the Disk

When you learn how to do programs in UNIX, you start with just one program file. Programs seem to grow on their own, however. First, you add a subprogram and then another. Because a program requires information, you may create a database file. You also eventually create different versions of your program as you make changes to it.

Keeping track of all the files necessary to run your programs is vitally important. How do programmers keep things organized, though? They create subdirectories in their home directory. Each of the programs you create should have its own subdirectory on your hard disk, to isolate it from other programs you're building.

To create a subdirectory, use the mkdir command:

```
mkdir payroll_proj
```

This line tells your computer to set aside a section of your disk and call it payroll_proj. In this area, you put all the files related to your payroll project.

You can access this new area of your hard disk by using the cd command. This command tells your computer to change to that directory:

```
cd payroll_proj
```

After the new directory is displayed, you can create other subdirectories. Each subdirectory houses a different type of file. The following example shows how a programmer typically organizes files for a program:

```
mkdir payroll_proj
mkdir payroll_proj/release_version
mkdir payroll_proj/version1
mkdir payroll_proj/data
mkdir payroll_proj/documents
```

When you start a new programming project, you should use the mkdir command to create a project directory as a branch of your home directory. This is what is happening in the first line of this example. The new programming project is called payroll, so I call the project directory payroll_proj to clearly identify the contents of this directory.

Beneath the payroll_proj directory are additional subdirectories that contain specific information about the project. I create four such subdirectories as branches of the payroll_proj directory. One of these subdirectories will contain the release version of the program. I call the subdirectory release_version. When I finish writing and testing my payroll program, I'll place the program in this directory so I'll always have a copy of the program ready for anyone who asks for the program.

The *release version* of the program is also called the *current version* of the program. Every time that you change the instructions in the program, you create a new version of the program. You are familiar with this concept with Windows, for example, which has a version 2.0, 3.0, 3.1. These are version numbers, and each one signifies that changes were made to the previous version of the program. To help me keep track of versions of my own program, I create a subdirectory for each version and then place the appropriate version of the program in that subdirectory. In this example, I have only one version of my program, so I need to create only one subdirectory called version1.

Two other subdirectories that programmers commonly create for new programming projects are for data and documentation. *Data* is the information that is needed by the program to complete the task. Frequently, this information is contained in a file on your hard disk — and stored in the data directory. Likewise, the documentation subdirectory is used to store files that contain instructions for the using the program and notes about the design of the program, such as flow charts.

This is just the typical subdirectory layout that I use when I begin a new programming project. It is important that you keep your program files organized and this example will give you a head start in creating your own subdirectory layout for your programming projects.

Changing the Characters in a File

This section presents a trick that can save you a great deal of programming time. If you ever have to perform a global search and replace for information in a file, you can do it by using the tr command. This command changes the information efficiently.

If you want to change all the lowercase letters in a data file to uppercase, for example, type this command:

```
tr "[a-z]" "[A-Z]" < dataInput > dataOutput
```

The first argument, "[a-z]", is the information your computer searches for.

The information that you want to replace the first argument in the file is shown in the second argument, "[A-Z]".

The third argument, dataInput, is the file to be searched.

The computer places the modified information in the dataOutput file, which is the last argument.

Check out the man pages (manual pages) on the tr command to learn more neat tricks:

```
man tr
```

Maintaining Your Code

To keep your programs and their related files safe in a professional way, save them in an archive file. An archive file is managed by the ar command and enables you to place several files under one name. It's like having a file drawer that contains all your programs and files. You can refer the label on the file drawer when you need to look at any of the files stored in the drawer. Except in this case, the file drawer is really an archive file that has its own name. Inside the archive file are all your other files that relate to your program.

Suppose that you're building the payroll program mentioned earlier in this chapter. The program consists of a program file and subprograms, data files, and documentation files.

You can organize these files by creating subdirectories, or you can save them in an archive file, by typing this command:

```
ar q payroll_lib payroll
```

The q command tells the computer to append the file *q*uickly to the library file. payroll_lib is the name of the library file, and payroll is the file that is placed in the library file.

Whenever you want to use the payroll file, you ask your computer to retrieve it from the library file:

```
ar x payroll_lib payroll
```

The x command tells the computer to extract the file from the library. When you're finished with the file, you return it to the library by using the r command:

```
ar r payroll_lib payroll
```

Pausing Your Program

You can have your program pause at any time by using the sleep command. This command temporarily stops the execution of your code until a specified number of seconds has passed:

```
echo "How do you get 4 elephants into a compact car?"
sleep 10
echo "Two in the front and two in the back."
```

In this example, your computer first asks a question and then is told to pause for ten seconds. Then the punch line is displayed (that's a sick one).

Part IX
Appendixes

The 5th Wave

By Rich Tennant

Re·al Pro·gram·mers

Real Programmers don't sleep - their systems just temporarily go down.

In this part . . .

*H*ere is some very useful information that's ready at your fingertips. This part contains a glossary that helps you understand terms used in UNIX and UNIX programming. Another appendix is devoted to sharpening your skills as a master of the vi text editor. Good luck. You also find here a handy cross-reference table that contains the keywords for the C shell, the Bourne shell, and the Korn shell. You can use this information to convert your C shell programs to the Bourne shell or the Korn shell. Wow. And finally I include lots of exercises — with the answers — to challenge your newly developed C shell programming skills.

Appendix A:
Glossary

● ●

anonymous FTP

Many computer systems allow anyone to log in as anonymous and then transfer files without having a formal user name on the computer. After connecting with the remote computer, you type anonymous in response to the user ID prompt; you then type your e-mail address as your password. The transfer of files is made possible through the use of the *file transfer program* (FTP).

application

A program that does real-world work, such as a payroll program or a word-processing program.

argument

Information that you enter on the command line alongside the name of the program. For example:

```
rm myfile
```

myfile is an argument to the program rm (which removes the file from your disk). An argument is information that is sent by UNIX to your program when your program begins.

background

Describes a program that runs in the background while other programs are running on your computer. Many programs can run at the same time in UNIX. Thus, some of those that require no interaction with you run behind the scenes (in the *background*).

backslash (\)

Used in UNIX to identify the character to the right of the backslash as a special character. For example:

```
\n
```

In this case, \n indicates a new line on the screen. Technically, the backslash tells UNIX to ignore the way you normally handle the next character and to treat it in a special way. (The normal way the n is handled by UNIX is to display the letter n on the screen.)

backup

An extra electronic copy of your program or data that you should keep in a safe place; you can use a backup to restore the program or data in case the information is erased.

bit

The smallest piece of information that your computer understands — and which is represented as a 1 or a 0. A bit is normally thrown together with seven other bits to form a byte.

Bourne shell

A program that allows you to enter commands into UNIX. It is the most widely used shell and has the $ as the prompt. You can begin the Bourne shell by typing the following at the prompt and pressing Enter:

```
sh
```

BSD UNIX

The version of UNIX that was developed by the University of California at Berkeley. BSD represents *B*erkeley *S*oftware *D*istribution.

buffer

A place in memory where information is temporarily stored until it is needed by a program. Text editors use buffers to store a copy of your file while you edit it; printers use buffers to store the file that is being printed.

byte

A collection of eight bits that is used to represent information. Eight bits enable 256 different combinations of eight 1s and 0s (256 is 2^8). Many computers use the ASCII code to translate characters on the keyboard to a unique pattern of 1s and 0s.

C Shell

A program that allows use to enter commands into UNIX. The C shell uses the % as the prompt. You can begin the C shell by typing the following at the prompt and pressing Enter:

```
csh
```

central processing unit (CPU)

The brains of the computer that performs all the "thinking" for the computer. Some command central processing units are the Pentium, SPARC, and 80486.

command

A word that you type at a shell prompt to direct UNIX to do something productive. Commands are names of things that the shell knows how to do. They are also names of programs that you or someone else writes using a shell script language.

command mode

A mode in a text editor where you enter commands. Pressing Esc when using vi, for example, places the text editor into the command mode.

CPU

See central processing unit.

current directory

See working directory.

current job

The job marked with a plus sign when you enter the job command at the shell prompt. A *job* is a program or command that is running.

cursor

A little character on the screen that indicates the current position on the screen. The actual character that appears on the screen varies on the program that you are using. Typically a flashing underscore character or box is used as the cursor.

daemon

Pronounced "demon." This is a program that runs in the background without requiring any input from you. Daemons perform housekeeping functions, such as printing files that are waiting in the queue.

data

Information that is used by UNIX or your program to complete a task. Your password is data to the program that must verify that you have access to the computer.

directory

A collection of files identified by a single name on your hard disk.

disk

A round, flat platter where information can be electronically stored in much the same way as your voice is recorded on an audio tape.

editor

See text editor.

Escape key

The key on your keyboard labeled Esc or Escape. The function of the Esc depends on the program that is running. For example, in the vi editor, Esc places vi in the command mode.

executable file

A file that UNIX can run. Executable files include programs and shell scripts.

external command

A program that has the same name as a shell command.

file

A hunk of information stored under the same name in memory or on your disk.

file system

The organization of files on your disk. A file system begins with the root directory and branches to many other directories called subdirectories. Files are stored in either the root directory or a subdirectory.

filter

A UNIX program that changes the way information in a file is displayed. For example, the sort program changes the order in which the information is displayed. The sort program is a filter.

foreground

A program that is running — you can talk to the program and the program can talk to you. Another way to run a program is in the background (where you can't talk to the program).

FTP (file transfer protocol)

A program that enables you to log in to a remote computer and transfer files to or from the remote computer. *See* anonymous FTP.

gateway

A connection between two different kinds of computer networks.

home directory

The directory that you are in after you log into your computer. Your home directory is usually a subdirectory of /usr.

input mode

A mode of a text editor during which time you can enter text. For example, in the vi text editor, pressing i when in the command mode places you in the insert mode.

I/O

Information going into your computer or program or leaving your computer or program (input/output).

job

A program that is running in a shell.

keyboard

The device you use to enter characters into your computer.

kill

A UNIX command that allows you to stop a program that is running. For example:

```
kill %payroll
```

This command stops the payroll program (and nobody gets paid!).

Korn shell

An improved version of the Bourne shell that uses the $ as the prompt. Type the following at the prompt and press Enter to begin the Korn shell:

```
ksh
```

line editor

A text editor that allows you to edit text one line at a time. The ed program is a line editor.

log in

The process of identifying yourself to the computer. This process requires you to enter a user ID and a password that UNIX validates before you can use the computer.

memory

A short-term storage area inside your computer where information is held temporarily (just while you're working on it). Your hard disk is used for long-term storage.

menu

A list of choices from which you can choose and have UNIX or your program perform a task.

Motif

A program that gives UNIX the look of Microsoft Windows. Motif is distributed by the Open Software Foundation and is based on the X Window System.

nerd

You, if you spend too much time working on your computer.

OPEN LOOK

A program that gives UNIX the look of Microsoft Windows, similar to Motif.

operating system

A program or group of programs that take over your computer's hardware and allow you to give your computer instructions to follow.

option

A symbol that tells a program or command to do something different than what it normally does. An option is sometimes called a *flag* or *switch*. For example, the command ls lists files in a directory. However, you can use an option — in this case -l — to make ls display an expanded list of information. You would type the following:

```
ls -l
```

parent directory

A directory that contains subdirectories.

password

A secret word that only you and your computer knows about (you hope). A combination of your user name and your secret password can gain you access to the computer.

pathname

A list of directories and subdirectories in which UNIX should look for programs that you tell UNIX to run. UNIX starts with the first directory on the pathname and, if the program isn't found, continues to look into all the directories/ subdirectories on the pathname until the program is found. If the program still isn't found after looking into all the specified directories/subdirectories, UNIX displays a message on the screen telling you that the program can't be located.

permissions

A list of symbols associated with a file or directory that specifies who has access to the file or directory. There are three kinds of permissions: read, write, and execute. The read and write permissions allow someone to read a file and write to a file. The execute permission allows someone to run the file, such as a program you've created.

pipe

Redirects the output of a command from the screen to input into another command. A pipe is symbolized with the | character. For example:

```
cat myfile | sort
```

This command redirects the display of the contents of myfile from the screen as input to the sort program.

process

A program that is running in UNIX.

prompt

The character that is shown on the screen in UNIX telling you that UNIX is waiting for you to do something. For example, with the C shell you would see this prompt:

```
%
```

read-only

A file that can be read and copied but not written or changed. This is one of the permissions that UNIX allows you to specify for a file or directory.

redirection

A way to change the normal flow of information into and out of a program. *See* pipe.

root directory

The top level directory on your hard disk. All other directories branch out from the root directory.

screen editor

A text editor that fills your entire screen with text of your file. The vi text editor is a screen editor.

shell

A program that let's you talk to UNIX, which in turn talks to your computer hardware.

shell script

A file containing a list of shell commands that can be run like a program.

slash (/)

The character used to separate directories and subdirectories in the pathname.

```
/payroll/year1996/myvacation
```

software

Programs that contain instructions that tell your computer to perform a task.

Solaris

A version of UNIX that is designed for use on a Sun workstation.

subdirectory

See directory.

superuser

A user who has the right to really mess up the computer — and do a lot of good things, too. A superuser is also known as the *root*.

switch

See option.

system administrator

The person who is responsible for keeping your computer and UNIX running.

System V

The version of UNIX developed by AT&T and later distributed by UNIX System Labs, which is part of Novell.

text editor

A program that enables you to create and edit files. One of the most popular UNIX text editors is vi (although many programmers hate to use it).

text file

A file that contains ASCII characters and no control characters. (Control characters are symbols used by word processors to make your text fancy, such as font and type size.)

UNIX

A multi-user processing system developed in 1972 at Bell Laboratories.

UNIX International (UI)

A group of vendors who support System V.

user name

The name that you enter when you log into UNIX. UNIX then compares your user name and password with its list of know users to determine if you can have access to the computer.

utility

A program that comes with UNIX and performs one task very well. For example, the cmp utility compares two files and tells you where these files differ. Find out about any utility by using the manual pages. For example, if you want to know more about cmp, type the following at the command prompt and press Enter:

```
man cmp
```

wildcard

A symbol that takes the place of any character when used in a filename or pathname. The two symbols used as wildcards in UNIX are * and ?.

working directory

The current directory that you are working in. You can use the pwd command to ask UNIX to tell you the name of the working directory.

X Window System (or just X)

A program that allows you to break UNIX into several windows on the screen. Each window is running a shell and permits you to run different programs in each window.

XENIX

A version of UNIX developed by Microsoft and distributed by the Santa Cruz Organization (SCO).

Appendix B

When The Moon Hits Your Eye Like a Big Piece of vi

● ●

*T*hroughout this book I've be telling you that, to create a UNIX program, you must type into your program file all the instructions necessary for the program to carry out the task you want it to.

You enter those instructions in your program file by using a text editor. Probably the most widely used text editor in UNIX (and sometimes the most hated because of the awkwardness of entering text editor commands) is called vi. (I even gave you a brief introduction to vi in Chapter 3.)

Although vi isn't normally discussed in a UNIX programming book (this topic is usually covered in a book about UNIX), I thought that you would benefit from a quick overview of how to use vi to write your programs. This will serve as your basic introduction to vi. And if you've used vi before, you'll find this a good review.

Become comfortable using vi, for you may find that this is the only text editor that is available on your copy of UNIX.

Launching vi

There are two ways to start up the vi editor. The first way is to simply type vi at the command line and press the Enter key. Here's how this is done (using the C shell — indicated by the % prompt — as an example):

```
% vi
```

This keyboard gymnastics results in vi opening an empty document on the screen. You have to give the document a name before you save the document to a file.

The other way to begin vi is to specify the name of the file when you start up vi. Say that you want to create a file called *myfirstprogram*. Here's what you type on the command line:

```
% vi myfirstprogram
```

The vi text editor first tries to find a file called myfirstprogram in your current directory. If the file is found, the first page of the file is displayed on the screen within the vi text editor. However, if the file isn't found, an empty page is displayed.

When you later want to save myfirstprogram to a file, you won't need to specify the name of the file because the vi text editor automatically saves your work with the name that you specified when you started vi.

No Mouse!

All of us face life's disappointments.

The vi text editor is primitive when compared to today's standards for text-editing programs. You won't find any conveniences that you expect to see with a word processor. For one thing, you can move you mouse all you want, but the vi text editor ignores it (how dare it!) unless you are running vi in an X Windows environment. (X Windows is software that allows you to have multiple windows on the screen at the same time.)

So you have to settle for using either the arrow keys or issuing one of the vi text editor commands to moves the cursor around the page.

You can avoid frustration when trying to move the cursor in the vi text editor by forgetting the way you move the cursor in other programs. The sooner that you become comfortable using the arrow keys or issuing the necessary vi text editor commands, the sooner you can start writing your UNIX program.

The Mode-ous Operandi of vi

The vi text editor interprets what you type in three different ways. At first contact, you'd think that you and the vi text editor are going to have difficulties communicating with each others. And it's true when you first begin using vi. However, after you practice awhile, you'll be on the right wave length to communicate with the vi text editor.

Here are the three modes:

- **Command mode:** Everything that you type on your keyboard is inter-preted as a command telling the vi text editor to do something. For example, pressing the letter **j** in the command mode tells the vi text editor to move the cursor down one line on the screen.

  Note: The vi text editor starts up in the command mode. You can also enter the command mode from any other mode at anytime by pressing Esc.

- **Input mode:** Everything that you type on your keyboard is placed on the page on the screen and in the file when you save the pages (just like a regular word processor does). For example, pressing the letter **j** while the vi text editor is in the input mode displays the letter **j** on the page at the cursor.

  You can enter the input mode from the command mode by pressing **i** or **a**. The letter i is the command to insert characters on the page at the cursor, and the letter a is the command to append characters to the page right after the cursor.

- **Last line mode:** Everything that you type on your keyboard in this mode is interpreted by the vi text editor as a last-line command. That is, the characters appear on the last line of the vi text editor at the bottom of your screen.

  You can enter the last line mode from the command mode by entering a colon (:). For example, you can press the letter **q** in the last line mode, which tells the vi text edtior to exit (quit).

Waiting for your command, sir

If you start the vi text editor without opening a previously saved file, you see a near empty page displayed on your screen; the left margin is filled with the tilde (~) character going down the page (see Figure B-1).

This look gives you the wrong impression that the tilde is the vi text editor's way of telling you where a line on the page begins. The tilde is really implying that these are *empty* lines. Avoid being confused that an empty line is a blank line. It isn't. An empty line means the line doesn't really exist — whereas a blank line means that the line exists but doesn't have any characters on the line.

Remember, the vi text editor starts up in the command mode: Anything that you type is interpreted as a command. This is quite different than other text editors such as Windows Notepad, which starts up in the insert mode. (Notepad doesn't even have a separate command mode!)

Not remembering this command mode versus input mode stuff is a common mistake many UNIX programmers make when they first start using the vi text editor. What happens is simple: The programmer begins typing away without looking at the screen. When he or she does glance at the screen, only part of the text appears. Why? Because as the programmer is typing, the vi text editor is in the command mode. Each letter is interpreted as a command — not as text. vi ignores most of the letters because the letters are not commands. However, as soon as the programmer enters an i, vi enters the insert mode, and then all the following letters are entered directly on the page.

Get me out of here!

You can exit the vi text editor using one of several commands. However, the fastest way is Press the Esc key to enter the command mode, and then press ZZ. This action saves any changes to the file that you've made and exits the vi text editor. If you haven't made any changes, the file won't be saved, but you still exit vi.

Moving Around Inside Your File

Here's a good way for you to learn the various vi commands that are used to get you around your files. Find a large text file on your hard disk. A text file is almost like a word-processing file, except those special symbols that control things like the font and size of the letters are missing from the file. Try to find a file called *readme* or *readme.txt* on your hard disk. These files are sometimes distributed with other software to keep you up-to-date on the latest changes that have occurred with the program.

However, if you can't find any text files, you can use vi to create one. Just begin vi; press i to enter the input mode; then type a whole bunch of lines on the page. Hey, why not just type some of the UNIX code that you see in this book? You may go on to other pages if you get carried away with your typing — but that's just fine.

Just line up

The vi text editor displays your text on lines shown on your screen. The cursor is automatically placed on the first character of the first line of the text. Each line of text (including those lines that can't fit on the screen but exist in the file) has a number. The first line is number 1, the second line is number 2 and so forth.

You can display the number of the line that the cursor is on by pressing Ctrl+G. I've done that in Figure B-2, where I have myfirstprogram open. Notice that the line number is indicated at the bottom of the screen. (The cursor is on line 3 of a 14-line file.)

```
set flag = "go"
while ($flag == "go")
   echo "Enter your name or type stop to end: "
   set friend = $<
   if ($friend == "stop") then
      set flag = "stop"
      break
   endif
   if ($friend == "Tom") then
      continue
   endif
   echo "Hello, $friend."
end
echo "Good-bye!"
~
~
~
~
~
~
~
~
~
"myfirstprogram" [Modified] line 3 of 14 --21%--
```

Figure B-2:
vi reveals
the line
number for
the cursor
position.

To see the line numbers alongside each line on the screen, as shown in Figure B-3, you can type **:set number** and press Enter when you are in the command mode. (This is really a command in last line mode, but you have to start in command mode.) Now you have the number for each line, which is an important navigational aid when you want to move around quickly in vi.

```
 1  set flag = "go"
 2  while ($flag == "go")
 3     echo "Enter your name or type stop to end: "
 4     set friend = $<
 5     if ($friend == "stop") then
 6        set flag = "stop"
 7        break
 8     endif
 9     if ($friend == "Tom") then
10        continue
11     endif
12     echo "Hello, $friend ."
13  end
14  echo "Good-bye!"
~
~
~
~
~
~
~
~
~
:set number
```

Figure B-3: Line numbers at a glance make for easy navigation.

You can move the cursor to any line in your text by using the command shown in Table B-1. Before you type any of these commands, make sure that vi is in the command mode by pressing the Esc key. You'll notice that the table contains the letter *n* in some of the commands. For example, say that you want to move the cursor to line 12 in your text. *n*G is the command that you use to tell the vi text editor to move to a particular line number. However, you must replace the letter *n* by the number of the line that you want. In this case, you type **12G** and press Enter. The cursor moves to the beginning of line 12 in your text. (In Figure B-4, I've done these very steps, and my cursor rests at the beginning of line 12.)

Keep in mind that the vi text editor commands are *case sensitive,* so where you see a capital letter as the command, you must use upper case. Likewise, if the command is shown in lowercase.

```
 1  set flag = "go"
 2  while ($flag == "go")
 3      echo "Enter your name or type stop to end: "
 4      set friend = $<
 5      if ($friend == "stop") then
 6          set flag = "stop"
 7          break
 8      endif
 9      if ($friend == "Tom") then
10          continue
11      endif
12      echo "Hello, $friend ."
13  end
14  echo "Good-bye!"
~
~
~
~
~
~
~
~
~
~
:set number
```

Figure B-4:
The cursor
has jumped
from line 3
to line 12.

Table B-1	Commands for Moving through Text by Line
Command	**What it does**
*n*G	Moves to the line that is specified. If no line is specified, the cursor is placed on the last line in the text.
H	Moves to the first line of the page shown on the screen
M	Moves to the middle line of the page shown on the screen
L	Moves to the last line of the page shown on the screen
n (↑) or *n*k	Moves up the number of lines that is specified while remaining in the same column of the line
n (↓)	Moves down the number of lines that is specified while remaining in the same column of the line
+ or Enter	Moves to the first nonwhite space on the next line. A nonwhite space is a character that you can see in your text. A white space character is a character that you can't see, such as a tab character.
−	Moves to the first nonwhite space on the previous line

Picking up speed

You can move around the text a lot faster than you can simply moving line by line. The vi text editor has another set of commands that you can use to move a screenful at a time. These are called screen-control commands and are shown in Table B-2.

A screenful, sometimes refered to as a *page,* is all the text that can appear on your screen at the same time. For example, in Windows you can fill your screen with a different part of your text by using the PgUp and PgDn keys or by using the vertical scroll bar.

However, these Windows methods won't work for you when you use the vi text editor. Instead, you must use the screen-control commands such as Ctrl+F to move to the next screen and Ctrl+B to move to the previous screen.

If you're using the vi text editor on a workstation (a computer that is between a mainframe computer and PC in terms of power), you may become confused as to what constitutes a screen. Some workstations have many windows (with X Windows) on the screen at the same time. Each window runs a different application, and one of those applications can be vi. In this case, the screen-control commands affect only the window showing the vi text editor. The other windows are not affected by these screen-control commands.

Table B-2	Screen Control Commands
Command	*What it does*
Ctrl+F	Moves to the next screen
Ctrl+B	Moves to the previous screen
Ctrl+D	Moves down half the current screen. You can enter the number of lines that you want to move down before pressing Ctrl+D to instruct the vi text editor to move down a specific number of line.
Ctrl+U	Moves up half the current screen — and as with Ctrl+D, you can specify the number of lines that you want to move down.
Ctrl+L	Clears the screen
z (press Enter)	Repaints the screen placing the current line at the top of the screen.
z.	Repaints the screen placing the current line at the middle of the screen.
Ctrl+E	Moves the screen down one line
Ctrl+Y	Moves the screen up one line

The word, sentence, and paragraph jump

You can fine tune your movements around your text by using the *word, sentence*, and *paragraph* commands. You need to be in the command mode for these to work. (Like you need to be told this again after reading this appendix.) Table B-3 contains a list of these additional commands.

Table B-3	Word, Sentence and Paragraph Commands
Command	*What It Does*
w	Moves forward one word
W	Moves forward one word that ends with a blank space
b	Moves back one word
B	Moves back one word that begins with a blank space
e	Moves to the end of the current word
E	Moves to the end of the current word that ends with a blank space
)	Moves to the beginning of the next sentence
(	Moves to the beginning of the previous sentence
}	Moves to the beginning of the next paragraph
}	Moves to the beginning of the previous paragraph
%	Finds the matching parenthesis (the cursor must be on a parenthesis for this command to work)

Just a character at a time

You can move the cursor throughout your text a character at a time by using the character commands of the vi text editor. Table B-4 shows you these commands.

Table B-4	Character Control Commands
Command	*What It Does*
^ (caret)	Places the cursor on the first nonwhite character on the current line
0 (zero)	Places the cursor at the beginning of the current line
$ (dollar sign)	Places the cursor at the end of the current line
l or → (or spacebar)	Moves the cursor right one character
h or ← (or Ctrl+H)	Moves the cursor left one character

I didn't mean that

You're bound to make a mistake or two when you use the vi text editor. Even professional UNIX programmers find themselves having to undo something they already entered into the text. There are two ways to do this:

- ✔ Press **u** to undelete anything that you've deleted using the *dd* or *x* command
- ✔ Press **U** to undelete the current line.

Around the text I searched for you

It is difficult to locate the character or word that you need in pages of text. This is especially true when you are trying to find a specific line in your UNIX program where the code is a jumble of UNIXese and English.

The vi text editor can come to your rescue when you find yourself in such a jam. You can command vi to locate the information that you need in your text. For example, say that you want to find the word "bye" in your program (and don't ask me why). You are, of course, in the command mode and ready to give some orders. You can then type **/bye** if you know that this word must be somewhere after your current cursor position. This command appears at the bottom of your screen, ready for you to press Enter. (See Figure B-5.)

After you press Enter, notice that the cursor jumps to the beginning of the search item — in this case the word bye, as shown in Figure B-6. (Of course, this demonstration is more impressive when you have a really big and confusing text, but you get the idea.)

```
 1   set flag = "go"
 2   while ($flag == "go")
 3      echo "Enter your name or type stop to end: "
 4      set friend = $<
 5      if ($friend == "stop") then
 6         set flag = "stop"
 7         break
 8      endif
 9      if ($friend == "Tom") then
10         continue
11      endif
12      echo "Hello, $friend ."
13   end
14   echo "Good-bye!"
~
~
~
~
~
~
~
~
/bye
```

Figure B-5:
vi is more than happy to search for you.

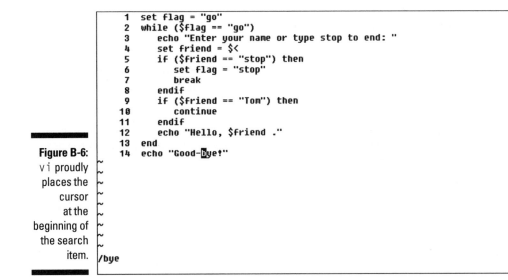

```
 1  set flag = "go"
 2  while ($flag == "go")
 3      echo "Enter your name or type stop to end: "
 4      set friend = $<
 5      if ($friend == "stop") then
 6          set flag = "stop"
 7          break
 8      endif
 9      if ($friend == "Tom") then
10          continue
11      endif
12      echo "Hello, $friend ."
13  end
14  echo "Good-Bye!"
~
~
~
~
~
~
~
~
/bye
```

Figure B-6: vi proudly places the cursor at the beginning of the search item.

Table B-5 contains the commands that you need to have vi conduct a search of your text or program.

Table B-5	Search Commands
Command	***What It Does***
/*pattern*	Begins the search from the cursor position for the characters that compose the pattern you are searching for (the word *pattern* in the command must be replaced with the characters or words that you are trying to locate in your text).
/*pattern*/+n	Places the cursor on the *n*th line after the line that contains the characters or words that you are searching for. (Replace *n* with the number of the line.) For example, /Bob/+3 places the cursor on the third line below the line where vi finds the word Bob.
?*pattern*	Begins the search at the cursor and continues to search backwards through the text
?*pattern*?–n	Places the cursor on the *n*th line before the line that contains the characters or words that you are searching for. For example, ?Bob?–3 places the cursor on the third line above the line where vi finds the word Bob.
n	Repeats the last / or ? command
N	Repeats the last / or ? command but reverses the direction of the search

Using the Input Mode

By now you've probably heard all you ever wanted to know about vi commands. Your sleeves are rolled up and you're ready to plow into inserting text into your page. However, before you can tackle this chore, you need to learn — what else? — a few more vi commands.

I begin by showing you the various ways for you to enter the input mode from the command mode. Table B-6 contains the commands that you need to know before you begin typing away.

Table B-6	Entering the Input Mode
Command	*What It Does*
a	Places new text after the cursor position
A	Places new text after the end of the current line
i	Places new text in front of the cursor position
I	Places new text in front of the current line
o	Places new text below the current line at the beginning of the next line
O (Capital O)	Places new text on the line above the current line at the beginning of the line
r	Replaces the character at the cursor with the next character entered at the keyboard. For example, rb replaces the character at the cursor with the letter b.
R	Overwrites the text beginning with the character over the cursor. You can stop overwriting the text by returning to the command mode (by pressing Esc).
cw*word*+Esc	Replaces the word at the cursor with another word. For example, if the cursor is on the word Bob and you enter cwMary and press Esc, vi replaces the word Bob with the word Mary.

Copy editing the vi way

The vi text editor has a wealth of editing commands that make it a breeze to change whatever you typed into your text. All these commands require that you place vi in the command mode by pressing Esc, otherwise all the commands that you type will be placed into your text. Table B-7 contains text-editing commands. (Be sure to replace *n* with a number.)

Table B-7	Text Editing Commands
Command	*What It Does*
*n*x	Deletes *n* characters beginning with the character at the cursor
*n*X	Deletes *n* characters backwards from the character at the cursor
D	Deletes the line from the cursor to the end of the line
dw	Deletes the word at the cursor position
dd	Deletes the line on which the cursor is located
J	Combines the line where the cursor is located with the next line. The next line is placed at the end of the current line.
. (period)	Repeats the previous editing command

Cut and paste text without scissors and glue

You're probably familiar with the cut and paste features of PCs running Windows and Macs. You highlight the text that you want cut, select Cut from the Edit menu, and the text disappears from the screen. Then, move the cursor to the spot in your text where you want the text to be inserted and select Paste from the Edit menu. Right before your eyes, the text that disappeared appears again.

The vi text editor has similar features called *yank* and *put*. Yank is the same as cut and put is the same as paste in Windows. Table B-8 contains the yank and put commands. (Replace *n* with a number.)

Table B-8	Yank and Put Commands
Command	*What It Does*
*n*yy	Removes *n* lines from the text and places those lines into your computer's memory
*n*yl	Removes *n* characters beginning with the character at the cursor and places those characters into your computer's memory
p	Places the yanked text after the cursor
P	Places the yanked text before the cursor

Using the Last Line Mode

The *last line mode* lets you read files into the vi text editor so you can edit them. This mode also lets you write files to a disk (just like saving a file) after you finish editing the file. And you use the last line mode to exit vi.

You can enter the last line mode by first placing vi in the command mode (by pressing Esc). After you are in the command mode, press the colon (:). This places vi in the last line mode.

All the commands that are entered in the last line mode appear at the bottom of the screen (and *that's* where the name comes from). After you enter the command, you must press Enter for the command to be executed. Table B-9 contains last line mode commands.

Table B-9	Last Line Mode Commands
Command	*What It Does*
r *filename*	Reads the file named in the command into the vi text editor and places the first character of the file at the current cursor position
e *filename*	Edits the file named in the command and stops editing the file currently in the vi text editor
e!	Discards changes made to the file since the file was last saved and begins to edit the file again
e#	Changes between the two files most recently edited. You must save the file that your editing before you can switch to the other file.

Practicing safe file editing

You can prevent yourself from catching the fatal disease that strikes many new UNIX programmers. It's called "I lost my files!" The disease hits you when you least expect it. You've spent hours typing away, entering code into your vi text editor. Then suddenly, without warning, you computer goes blank. It's like someone turned off the power switch and all your hard work is lost forever.

The best defense against this disease is protection. Always save your files regularly while your working on your files in vi. Table B-10 shows you the save file commands.

Note: You must be in the last line mode for these commands to work. First, be sure that you are in the command mode by pressing Esc, and then type a colon (:) followed by the command.

Table B-10	Save File Commands
Command	*What It Does*
w	Writes the current file to disk and overwrites the contents of the copy of the file that is on the disk
w *filename*	Writes the current file to disk using the file name that you specify in the command. Be sure to replace *filename* with the name of the file that you want to use for the current file.
w! filename	Writes the current file to disk using the file name that you specify in the command — and overwrites the contents of the copy of the file that is on disk

Bailing out of vi

Stop, already. Here are some ways to exit the vi text editor. All these commands require vi to be in the last line mode, and you must press Enter to execute the command. Table B-11 contains exit commands for the vi text editor.

You can simply press ZZ in the command mode (without pressing enter) to exit vi and save changes to your file.

Table B-11	Exit Commands
Command	*What It Does*
:q	Exits vi only if changes that you made to the file being edited are saved to the disk
:q!	Exits vi regardless if you've saved changes to the file to the disk
:x	Has the same affect as the ZZ command

Appendix C
Shell Conversion

• •

How to Use This List

Throughout this book, I show you how to write a program using the C shell. However, you may want to try your programming skills with the Bourne shell or the Korn shell, both very popular UNIX shells. (The Bourne shell and C shell are found in most versions of UNIX; the Korn shell is found in many but not all versions of UNIX.) This list helps you to get up to speed with the Bourne and Korn shells. After you write your program using the techniques that you learned in this book, you can match the C shell keywords with the Bourne shell or Korn shell equivalents. You'll soon notice that the Bourne shell and the Korn shell commands are usually similar — and all three shells sometimes have the same command.

Note: This list is by no means exhaustive. And some commands in the Bourne shell and the Korn shell have no equivalents in the C shell. I won't even get into that now!

Starting the shell from a program

C shell	Bourne shell	Korn shell
#!/bin/csh	/bin/sh	/bin/ksh

Setting a variable

C shell	Bourne shell and Korn shell
set variable	variable =

Resetting a variable

C shell	Bourne shell and Korn shell
unset variable	unset variable

Referring to a string variable

C shell	Bourne shell and Korn shell
$variable	$variable

Picking out data from a string array

C shell	**Bourne shell and Korn shell**
| ```
set var =(1 2 3 4)
echo $var[1]
``` | ```
var[1]=100
echo $var[1]
``` |

The if *statement*

C shell	**Bourne shell and Korn shell**
| ```
if (condition) then
   command
endif
``` | ```
if condition
then
   command
fi
``` |

The if else *statement*

C shell	**Bourne shell and Korn shell**
| ```
if (condition) then
   command
else
   command
endif
``` | ```
if condition
then
   command
else condition
   command
fi
``` |

The if else if *statement*

C shell	**Bourne shell and Korn shell**
| ```
if (condition) then
   command
elseif (condition)
   command
else
   command
endif
``` | ```
if condition
then
   command
elif condtion
   command
else
   command
fi
``` |

The switch case *statement*

C shell	**Bourne shell and Korn shell**
| ```
switch
case value:
   command
   breaksw
default
   command
endsw
``` | ```
case variable in
value)
   command
   ;;
*)
esac
``` |

The while *loop*

C shell	**Bourne shell and Korn shell**
| ```
while (condition)
  commands
end
``` | ```
while condition
do
    commands
done
``` |

Breaking out of a loop

C shell	**Bourne shell and Korn shell**
break	break
(to break out of the foreach and while loops)	(to break out of the for, while, and until loops)

Resuming a loop

C shell	**Bourne shell and Korn shell**
continue	continue
(to resume next iteration for the while loop)	(to resume next iteration for the for or while loops)

The foreach *loop*

C shell	**Bourne shell and Korn shell**
| ```
foreach variable
(item1 item2)
  command
end
``` | ```
for i [in list]
do
    command
done
```
(executes command between do and done by substituting the $i with each item in the list. in list contains the values that are assigned to $i.) |

## *Making UNIX wait (suspends script for n seconds)*

| **C shell** | **Bourne shell and Korn shell** |
|---|---|
| sleep n | sleep n |

## *Appending standard output to a file*

| **C shell** | **Bourne shell and Korn shell** |
|---|---|
| >> file | >> file |

### Taking standard input from a file

| C shell | Bourne shell and Korn shell |
|---------|------------------------------|
| `< file` | `< file` |

### Sending standard output to a file

| C shell | Bourne shell and Korn shell |
|---------|------------------------------|
| `> file` | `> file` |

### Equal to

| C shell | Bourne shell | Korn shell |
|---------|--------------|------------|
| `==` | `-eq` | `-eq (or ==)` |

### Not equal to

| C shell | Bourne shell | Korn shell |
|---------|--------------|------------|
| `!=` | `-ne` | `-ne (or !=)` |

### Less than

| C shell | Bourne shell | Korn shell |
|---------|--------------|------------|
| `<` | `-lt` | `-lt (or <)` |

### Less than or equal

| C shell | Bourne shell | Korn shell |
|---------|--------------|------------|
| `<=` | `-le` | `-le (or <=)` |

### Greater than

| C shell | Bourne shell | Korn shell |
|---------|--------------|------------|
| `>` | `-gt` | `-gt (or >)` |

### Greater than or equal to

| C shell | Bourne shell | Korn shell |
|---------|--------------|------------|
| `>=` | `-ge` | `-ge (or >=)` |

# Appendix D

# UNIX Programming Exercises

● ● ● ● ● ● ● ● ● ● ● ● ● ● ● ● ● ● ● ● ● ● ● ● ● ● ● ● ● ● ● ● ● ● ● ● ● ● ● ● ● ● ●

*N*o more multiple-choice tests with outrageously wrong answers to help you locate the correct answer! Now you have to actually put your knowledge to use in order to solve the exercises in this appendix. But don't fear! This is an open-book activity — and the answers are provided right after the question. You can peek if you want.

*Note:* I group the exercises by chapter, but not all the chapters have corresponding exercises.

## Chapter 3: Writing Your First UNIX Program

**1. How do you start the** vi **text editor?**

Type vi followed by the name of the file that you want to create or modify.

```
vi myfile
```

2. What is the first line in a C shell program?

```
#!/bin/csh
```

3. What is the second instruction you should give the computer in most programs that you write?

```
clear
```

This command clears the screen of characters that are left over from the preceding program.

4. Write a program that displays the name Bob Smith **on the screen.**

```
#!/bin/csh
echo "Bob Smith"
```

5. Make a program called myprogram **into an executable program.**

```
chmod  777 myprogram
```

Chapter 4: Using Variables

1. **Say that you want to write a UNIX program to keep track of your personal telephone list. Before you can solve this problem, you need to list all the pieces of information that you need to create the telephone list. What information would you include?**

   Answer: First name, last name, street, city, state, zip, home phone.

2. **Each piece of information on your list in the preceding exercise is identified in your program as a variable. Write down possible names of the variables that you would use for each piece of information on your list. (Remember the guidelines for naming UNIX files.)**

   Answer: FName, LName, Street, City, State, Zip, Hphone.

   Of course, your names may vary somewhat.

3. **Which of these piece(s) of information could be used to look up a telephone number?**

   Answer: LName, FName.

4. **Write the instruction that tells the computer to assign the name Bob to the FName variable.**

   ```
   set FName = "Bob"
   ```

5. **Write the instruction that tells the computer to declare the FName and LName variables without assigning a value to these variables.**

   ```
   set FName, Lname
   ```

Chapter 5: Interacting with the User

1. **Write a program that prompts someone to enter his or her name using the keyboard, and then have the program read the keyboard.**

```
#!/bin/csh
clear
echo "Enter your name"
set response = $<
```

2. **Modify the program in the preceding exercise so that a personal greeting is displayed on the screen. Change the program to display** Hello, **and then name the person entered at the keyboard.**

```
#!/bin/csh
clear
echo "Enter your name"
set response = $<
echo "Hello $response"
```

3. **Write a program that asks a person how much money he or she would like to make this year.**

```
#!/bin/csh
clear
echo "How much money would you like to make this year?"
@ salary  = $<
```

4. **Modify the program in the preceding exercise. Add 100 to whatever amount the person enters into the keyboard.**

```
#!/bin/csh
clear
echo "How much money would you like to earn this year?"
@ salary  = $<
@ salary = $salary + 100
```

5. **Modify the preceding program. Display a message on the screen saying "I think you will earn ___", and then display the amount they entered plus 100.**

```
#!/bin/csh
clear
echo "How much money would you like to earn this year?"
@ salary  = $<
@ salary = $salary + 100
echo "I think you will earn $salary"
```

Chapter 6: Arithmetic, Logical, and Comparison Operators

1. Write an expression that asks the computer if the values of two variables are the same.

```
$Var1 == $Var2
```

2. Write an expression that asks the computer if the values of two variables are different.

```
$Var1 != $Var2
```

3. Write an expression that asks the computer to add the values of two variables and assign the sum to another variable.

```
@ Var3 = $Var1 + $Var2
```

4. Write an expression that asks the computer to divide the values of two variables and assign the results to another variable.

```
@ Var3 = $Var1 \ $Var2
```

5. Write an expression that asks the computer to determine if the value of the variable SALARY is greater than $30,000.

```
$SALARY > 30000
```

Chapter 7: Using Comments

1. **Modify the following program by explaining (in the program) what the** echo **command does.**

```
#!/bin/csh
echo "Bob Smith"
```

Answer:

```
#!/bin/csh
#The echo command displays the name on the screen.
echo "Bob Smith"
```

2. **Modify the following program to include comments for each action the program must take.**

```
#!/bin/csh
clear
echo "How much money would you like to earn this year?"
@ salary  = $<
@ salary = $salary + 100
echo "I think you will earn $salary"
```

Answer:

```
#!/bin/csh
#clear the screen
clear
# prompt the user to enter a salary
echo "How much money would you like to earn this year?"
#read characters from the keyboard
@ salary  = $<
# add 100 to the value of the salary variable and assign
        the new value to the salary variable.
set @ salary = $salary + 100
#display the message and salary on the screen
echo "I think you will earn $salary"
```

3. **Give two ways that you can add a comment about this instruction:**
   @ salary = $<

   Answer: By placing the comment on the line above the instruction:

   ```
   #read characters from the keyboard
   @ salary  = $<
   ```

   Answer: By placing the comment on the same line but to the right of the instruction:

   ```
   @ salary  = $< #read characters from the keyboard
   ```

4. **How can *pseudo* code be used as comments for your program? (Yes, this is an essay question!)**

   Answer: You can list instructions that are necessary to complete a task as pseudo code (that's to say, the instructions written in real *English*) in your program file. UNIX, of course, does not understand English. However, you can place a number sign (#) as the first character of the pseudo code, which converts the pseudo code into a comment.

Chapter 8: The `if`, `if else`, and `if else if` Statements

1. **Write an** `if` **statement that displays the message** `Higher` **if the value of** `SALARY` **is lower than 30,000.**

```
if ($SALARY < 30000) then
    echo "Higher"
endif
```

2. **Write an** `if` **statement that displays the personal greeting** `Hello, Bob` **if the FName variable has the value** `Bob`**. Otherwise, display the message** `You're not Bob`**.**

```
if ($FName == "Bob") then
    echo "Hello, Bob"
else
    echo "You're not Bob"
endif
```

3. **Modify the following program from the first exercise. Write an instruction that tells the computer to display** `Higher` **if** `$SALARY` **is less than 30,000 and display** `Lower` **if the** `$SALARY` **is greater than 30,000.**

```
if ($SALARY < 30000) then
    echo "Higher"
endif
```

Answer:

```
if ($SALARY < 30000) then
    echo "Higher"
else if ($SALARY > 30000) then
    echo "Lower"
endif
```

4. **Modify the preceding program so that the message** Right On **is displayed if** $SALARY **is equal to 30000.**

```
if ($SALARY < 30000) then
    echo "Higher"
else if ($SALARY > 30000) then
    echo "Lower"
else
    echo "Right On"
endif
```

5. **Write an** if **statement that displays the message** Right On **if** $SALARY **is 30,000. However, you can't use the == operator (**$SALARY == 30000**). You must use the less than operator (<) and the greater than operator (>) in a single expression.**

```
if ($SALARY > 29999 && $SALARY <30001) then
    echo "Right On"
endif
```

Chapter 9: The `switch case` *Statement*

1. **Write a** `switch case` **statement that displays** `New York`, `Chicago`, `Boston` **if the value of the variable** `$city` **has the corresponding value.**

```
switch ($city)
    case  "New York" :
        echo "New York"
        breaksw
    case  "Chicago" :
        echo "Chicago"
        breaksw
    case  "Boston" :
        echo "Boston"
        breaksw
endsw
```

2. **Modify the** `switch` **statement from the preceding exercise to display** `Incorrect city entered.` **when none of the cities are selected.**

```
switch ($city)
    case  "New York" :
        echo "New York"
        breaksw
    case  "Chicago" :
        echo "Chicago"
        breaksw
    case  "Boston" :
        echo "Boston"
        breaksw
     default:
        echo "Incorrect city entered."
endsw
```

3. **Write instructions to have the computer display the following menu items. (Be sure to include a menu item to quit running the program.)**

   a) Search by name

   b) Search by telephone number

   c) Search by employee number

Answer:

```
echo "a) Search by name"
echo "b) Search by telephone number"
echo "c) Search by employee number"
echo "q) Quit"
```

4. **Modify the program in the preceding exercise and include instructions that tell the user to make a selection from the menu; include instructions to have the program read the user's selection from the keyboard.**

```
echo "a) Search by name"
echo "b) Search by telephone number"
echo "c) Search by employee number"
echo "q) Quit"
echo " "
echo "Enter your selection: "
set selection = <$
```

5. **Modify the program in the preceding exercise to include instructions that determine which selection was made by the user and display the name of the selection on the screen.**

```
echo "a) Search by name"
echo "b) Search by telephone number"
echo "c) Search by employee number"
echo "q) Quit"
echo " "
echo "Enter your selection: "
set selection = <$
switch ($response)
    case "a" :
        echo "Search by name"
        breaksw
    case "b" :
        echo "Search by telephone number"
        breaksw
    case "c" :
        echo "Search by employee number"
        breaksw
```

(continued)

(continued)

```
    case  "q" :
        echo "Quit"
        breaksw
    default:
        echo "Incorrect menu selection."
endsw
```

Chapter 11: The while Loop

1. **Write a program using a** while **loop that continues to add 1 the** $sum **variable until the** $sum **variable equals 10.**

```
@ sum = 0
while ($sum < 10)
    @ sum = $sum + 1
end
```

2. **Modify the program in the preceding exercise so the computer displays the current value of the** $sum **variable each time the value is incremented.**

```
@ sum = 0
while ($sum < 11)
    @ sum = $sum + 1
    echo "$sum"
end
```

3. **Modify the program in the first exercise so that the computer displays the message "sum is equal to 10" only when this is true.**

```
@ sum = 0
while ($sum < 11)
    @sum = $sum + 1
    if ($sum == 10) then
        echo "sum is equal to 10"
    endif
end
```

4. **In exercise 5 from Chapter 10, you built a program that displays a menu, prompts the user to enter a selection, reads the selection the user enters from the keyboard, and then displays the selection on the screen. Modify this program (given here) with a** while **loop so that the program continues until the user selects** q **to quit the program.**

Here's the original program:

```
echo "a) Search by name"
echo "b) Search by telephone number"
echo "c) Search by employee number"
echo "q) Quit"
echo " "
echo "Enter your selection: "
set selection = <$
switch ($response)
    case "a" :
        echo "Search by name"
        breaksw
    case "b" :
        echo "Search by telephone number"
        breaksw
    case "c" :
        echo "Search by employee number"
        breaksw
    case "q" :
        echo "Quit"
        breaksw
     default:
        echo "Incorrect menu selection."
endsw
```

Answer:

```
set flag = "1"
while ($flag == "1")
   clear
   echo "a) Search by name"
   echo "b) Search by telephone number"
   echo "c) Search by employee number"
   echo "q) Quit"
   echo " "
   echo "Enter your selection: "
   set selection = <$
```

```
    switch ($city)
        case "a" :
            echo "Search by name"
            breaksw
        case  "b" :
            echo "Search by telephone number"
            breaksw
        case  "c" :
            echo "Search by employee number"
            breaksw
        case  "q" :
            set flag = "0"
            breaksw
        default:
            echo "Incorrect menu selection."
    endsw
end
```

5. Create an endless while **loop that alternates displaying the message** Green **and** Red **on the screen.**

```
set flag = "1"
@ color = 0
while ($flag == "1")
    if ($color == 0) then
        clear
        @ color = 1
        echo "Green"
    endif
    if ($color == 1) then
        clear
        @ color = 0
        echo "Red"
    endif
end
```

Chapter 12: The `foreach` *Loop*

1. **Write a program that uses the** `foreach` **loop to display the cities that you travel to during your vacation. These cities are Paris, Rome, and London. (Bon voyage!)**

```
foreach city (Paris Rome London)
     echo "$city"
end
```

2. **Use a** `foreach` **loop to display a personal greeting to your friends Bob, Mary, and Joan.**

```
foreach friend (Bob Mary Joan)
     echo "Hi, $friend"
end
```

3. **Modify the preceding program to include the person's first and last name: Bob Smith, Mary Jones, Joan Adams.**

```
foreach friend ("Bob Smith" "Mary Jones" "Joan Adams")
     echo "Hi, $friend"
end
```

4. **Write a** `foreach` **loop that displays the message on one line** `Here is my friend` **— and on the second line identify your friends by name, using the names Bob Smith, Mary Jones, Joan Adams.**

```
foreach friend ("Bob Smith" "Mary Jones" "Joan Adams")
     echo "Here is my friend"
     echo "Hi, $friend"
end
```

5. **Modify the** `foreach` **loop of the preceding program so that you display the message** `She's great!` **only if Mary Jones is assigned to** `$friend`.

```
foreach friend ("Bob Smith" "Mary Jones" "Joan Adams")
     echo "Here is my friend"
     echo "Hi, $friend"
     if ($friend == "Mary Jones") then
        echo "She's great!"
     endif
end
```

Chapter 13: Nested Loops and Quick Exits

1. **Write a program that asks someone to enter his or her name, and then end the program only if the person enters the word** stop.

   Hint: Use the break **keyword to end the loop in the program.**

   ```
   #!/bin/csh
   set flag = "go"
   while ($flag == "go")
        clear
        echo "Enter your name or type stop to end: "
        set friend = $<
        if ($friend == "stop") then
             break
        endif
   end
   ```

2. **Modify the preceding program to have the computer return to the top of the loop if the person enters the name** Tom.

   Hint: Use the continue **keyword.**

   ```
   #!/bin/csh
   set flag = "go"
   while ($flag == "go")
      clear
      echo "Enter your name or type stop to end: "
      set friend = $<
      if ($friend == "stop")then
        break
      endif
      if ($friend == "Tom")then
        continue
      endif
   end
   ```

3. **Modify the preceding program so that a personal greeting is displayed only if the user does not enter the name** Tom **and does not enter the word** stop.

```
#!/bin/csh
set flag = "go"
while ($flag == "go")
    clear
    echo "Enter your name or type stop to end: "
    set friend = $<
    if ($friend == "stop")then
       break
    endif
    if ($friend == "Tom")then
       continue
    endif
    echo "Hello, $friend ."
end
```

4. **Write a program using the** `if` **statement to determine if a last name is Smith, and then determine if the first name is Bob. If they match, say "Hello" to Bob Smith on the screen.**

Hint: Use nested `if` **statements.**

```
#!/bin/csh
set fname = "Bob"
set lname = "Smith"
if (lname == "Smith" then
    if (fname == "Bob") then
       echo "Hello Bob Smith"
    endif
endif
```

5. **Write a program that displays "<name> has these <degree> degrees" but substitute Bob, Mary, and Joan for <name> and BS, MS, and Ph.D. for <degree>.**

Hint: Use a nested `foreach` **loop.**

```
#!/bin/csh
foreach name (Bob Mary Joan)
        foreach degree (BS MS Ph.D.)
             echo "$name has these $degree degrees"
        end
end
```

Chapter 14: Subprograms (That Everyone Can Share)

1. **Create a subprogram called** greeting **that displays** Hello, **and then create a program to call the greeting subprogram.**

   Program:

   ```
   #!/bin/csh
   greeting
   ```

   Subprogram: greeting

   ```
   echo "Hello"
   ```

2. **Write a subprogram called** addition **that adds 5 and 6 and then displays the results on the screen. Create a program to call the subprogram.**

   Program:

   ```
   #!/bin/csh
   addition
   ```

   Subprogram: addition

   ```
   @ sum = 5 + 6
   echo "$sum"
   ```

3. **Write a subprogram called** name **that displays** Bobby. **Write a program that displays** Hello **and then calls the subprogram.**

   Program:

   ```
   #!/bin/csh
   echo "Hello"
   name
   ```

   Subprogram: name

   ```
   echo "Bobby"
   ```

4. Modify the programming in the preceding exercise to display He's my friend. **after the name** Bobby.

Hint: The subprogram should only display the name Bobby.

Program:

```
#!/bin/csh
echo "Hello"
name
echo "He's my friend."
```

Subprogram: name

```
echo "Bobby"
```

5. Modify the preceding exercise so that the words He's my friend **are displayed by a second subprogram (called** name2**).**

Program:

```
#!/bin/csh
echo "Hello"
name
name2
```

Subprogram: name

```
echo "Bobby"
```

Subprogram: name2

```
echo "He's my friend."
```

Chapter 15: Passing and Accepting Arguments

1. **Write a program that accepts a person's name as an argument and then displays the name on the screen.**

   Call the program:

   ```
   name Bob
   ```

   Program: name

   ```
   #!/bin/csh
   echo "$argv[1]"
   ```

2. **Modify the program in the preceding exercise to accept and display the person's first and last name.**

   Call the program:

   ```
   name Bob Smith
   ```

   Program: name

   ```
   #!/bin/csh
   echo "$argv[1] $argv[2]"
   ```

3. **Modify the preceding exercise to accept the first and last name as one argument.**

   Call the program:

   ```
   name "Bob Smith"
   ```

   Program: name

   ```
   #!/bin/csh
   echo "$argv[1]"
   ```

4. **Modify the following program and subprogram so that the name displayed by the subprogram is received by the subprogram as an argument.**

   Program:

   ```
   #!/bin/csh
   echo "Hello"
   name
   ```

Subprogram: name

```
echo "Bobby"
```

Here are the answers:

Program:

```
#!/bin/csh
echo "Hello"
name Bobby
```

Subprogram: name

```
echo "$argv[1]"
```

5. **Modify the following program and subprogram so that the information displayed by both subprograms are passed as arguments to the subprograms.**

Program:

```
#!/bin/csh
echo "Hello"
name
name2
```

Subprogram: name

```
echo "Bobby"
```

Subprogram: name2

```
echo "He's my friend."
```

Here are the answers:

Program:

```
#!/bin/csh
echo "Hello"
name Bobby
name2 "He's my friend."
```

Subprogram: name

```
echo "$argv[1]"
```

Subprogram: name2

```
echo "$argv[1]"
```

Chapter 16: Using Database Files

1. **Write a program that saves the string** Hello World **to the file called** myfile.

```
#!/bin/csh
echo "Hello World" > myfile
```

2. **Write a program that saves the name** John Smith **to the file** myfile **and then appends the name** Mary Jones **to the same file.**

```
#!/bin/csh
echo "John Smith" > myfile
echo "Mary Jones" >> myfile
```

3. **How would you run the program** greeting **so that the output of the program prints to the file** myfile?

```
greeting > myfile
```

4. **Repeat the preceding exercise, however, and append the output of the program** greeting **to the file** myfile.

```
greeting >> myfile
```

5. **Write a program that saves the following information to the file** mydata. **Then use the** awk **utility to find and display the information for** Mary Jones.

Bob Smith 555-1212

Mary Jones 555-5555

Tom Adams 555-7777

John Smith 555-4444

```
#!/bin/csh
echo "Bob Smith 555-1212" >> mydata
echo "Mary Jones 555-5555" >> mydata
echo "Tom Adams 555-7777" >> mydata
echo "John Smith 555-4444" >> mydata
awk '$2 ~ /^Jones/ {print $1, $2, $3}' mydata
```

Chapter 17: Making Your Program Print Stuff Out

1. Send the words `Hello world` **to the printer.**

```
echo "Hello world" | lp
```

2. Print the following data to the printer.

Bob Smith 555-1212

Mary Jones 555-5555

Tom Adams 555-7777

John Smith 555-4444

```
echo "Bob Smith 555-1212" | lp
echo "Mary Jones 555-5555" | lp
echo "Tom Adams 555-7777" | lp
echo "John Smith 555-4444" | lp
```

3. Write the data in the preceding exercise to a file named `mydata`, **and then print the contents of the file.**

```
echo "Bob Smith 555-1212" >> mydata
echo "Mary Jones 555-5555" >> mydata
echo "Tom Adams 555-7777" >> mydata
echo "John Smith 555-4444" >> mydata
cat mydata | lp
```

4. How can you print a formatted file (that's to say, change fonts)?

Use a UNIX utility such as `troff`, which allows you to specify margins, fonts, and other formats for text that is being printed.

5. Modify the following program so that data selected by the `awk` **utility is printed rather than displayed on the screen.**

Here's the problem:

```
#!/bin/csh
echo "Bob Smith 555-1212" >> mydata
echo "Mary Jones 555-5555" >> mydata
echo "Tom Adams 555-7777" >> mydata
echo "John Smith 555-4444" >> mydata
awk '$2 ~ /^Jones/ {print $1, $2, $3}'mydata
```

Here's the answer:

```
#!/bin/csh
echo "Bob Smith 555-1212" >> mydata
echo "Mary Jones 555-5555" >> mydata
echo "Tom Adams 555-7777" >> mydata
echo "John Smith 555-4444" >> mydata
awk '$2 ~ /^Jones/ {print $1, $2, $3}'mydata | lp
```

Chapter 18: Stamping Out Bugs

1. What is the problem with the following code?

```
#!/bin/csh
clear
set name = "Bob"
if ($name == "Tom)
    echo "Hello Tom"
endif
```

Answer: The `if` statement is missing the `then` keyword.

2. What is the problem with the following code?

```
#!/bin/csh
clear
set name = "Bob"
while $name == "Tom"
    echo "Hello Tom"
end
```

Answer: The expression `$name == "Tom"` must be enclosed within parentheses:

```
while ($name == "Tom")
```

3. What is the problem with the following code?

```
#!/bin/csh
clear
set name = "Bob"
if ($name == "Tom") then
    echo "Hello Tom"
    if ($name != "Tom") then
        echo "You're not Tom."
endif
```

Answer: There are actually two problems. The second `if` statement will never run because the condition requires that the `$name` not be "Tom" — however, the `if` statement is nested inside another `if` statement that is executed only if the `$name` is "Tom". The second `if` statement is missing the `endif` keyword.

4. What is the problem with the following code? (Have you noticed a pattern with the questions for this set of exercises?)

```
#!/bin/csh
clear
switch ($city)
     case  "a" :
        echo "Search by name"
        breaksw
     case  "b" :
        echo "Search by telephone number"
        breaksw
     case  "c" :
        echo "Search by employee number"
        breaksw
     case  "q" :
        set flag = "0"
        breaksw
     default:
        echo "Incorrect menu selection."
  endsw
```

Answer: No value is assigned to $city. And the switch statement requires the end keyword — which is missing from the last line of this program.

5. What is the problem with the following code?

```
#!/bin/csh
clear
foreach friend (Bob Smith Mary Jones Joan Adams)
     echo "Hi, $friend"
end
```

Answer: The names Bob Smith and Mary Jones and Joan Adams should be enclosed within quotation marks:

```
foreach friend ("Bob Smith" "Mary Jones" "Joan Adams")
```

Index

• C •